Francis William Newman

Hebrew theism

The common basis of Judaism, Christianity and Mohammedism

Francis William Newman

Hebrew theism
The common basis of Judaism, Christianity and Mohammedism

ISBN/EAN: 9783337259730

Printed in Europe, USA, Canada, Australia, Japan

Cover: Foto ©Lupo / pixelio.de

More available books at **www.hansebooks.com**

HEBREW THEISM:

THE COMMON BASIS

OF

JUDAISM, CHRISTIANITY,

AND

MOHAMMEDISM,

WITH REVISIONS AND ADDITIONS TO THE QUARTO
EDITION OF 1858.

BY

FRANCIS W. NEWMAN.

"God is love"—*Epistle of John.*

"Of a truth I perceive that God is no respecter of persons; but in every nation he that feareth him and worketh righteousness is accepted with him."—*Peter, in the Acts.*

"In that day the Lord of Hosts shall say: Blessed be Egypt my people, and Assyria the work of my hands, and Israel mine inheritance.—*Isaiah.*

"Now abideth Faith, Hope, Love, these three; but the greatest of these is Love."—*Paul to the Corinthians.*

LONDON:
TRÜBNER AND CO., 57 & 59, LUDGATE HILL.

MDCCCLXXIV.

NOTTINGHAM:
STEVENSON, BAILEY, AND SMITH,
PRINTERS.

PREFACE.

A SECOND Edition of this Work makes me anxious to improve it as I best can; for it is hardly probable that I can live to a Third Edition. The improvement which I most seek, is the avoiding to build upon anything unsolid, or to overstate the certainty of any probable doctrine. I have added the seven sections, entitled, The Doubter, Historical Warnings, Freedom from Error, Happiness, Utilitarianism, Murder, Food and Drink. I have re-written and transposed the section on Free Will, and have now entitled it Praise and Blame. In the Third Book I have omitted one section, because the topic was too wide and difficult, and I had treated it partially. Throughout I have made small corrections, with occasional slight omission or addition.

The form and the style of this Book has not been adopted through affectation, or any love of novelty, but from the pressure of my problem itself. No one who has not essayed it, can know its difficulty. To expound the basis of religion much consecutive argument is wanted, and some metaphysics and logic; which is to be made intelligible and acceptable to a wholly unscientific public. A periodical style, with pronouns of reference (which, it) often recurring, and complex grammar, is notoriously ill-suited to the elements of Geometry. To make consecutive reasoning clear, the sentences must be very simple, the pronouns must be economized, and nouns re-iterated; and we know that all pleasure of style vanishes in Euclid. Like the Roman Lucretius in commending his philosophy to an unphilosophic public, I found no way of avoiding flatness and dryness, when I had made the sentences simple enough, but by a tinge of poetry; and to make poetical diction natural, something of poetical rhythm is essential. I do not expect to please the taste of scientific readers, but neither do I write for them. I am seeking to commend accurate logic to less austere minds; and after sixteen years' trial, I am confirmed in the belief that I have not misjudged.

In this Edition I have prefixed the epithet Hebrew to the title "Theism." I was too late in observing that *Greek Theism* is a more appropriate name for the doctrine which teaches, that God is moral but is in no moral relation to *individuals;* which doctrine, in the section entitled "Alternatives," I have reckoned as a form of Pantheism. In contrast to it the doctrine of this whole Volume is undoubtedly the *Hebrew* Theism.

December, 1873.

CONTENTS.

BOOK I.

Prologus 1	Law and Mercy 42
Animal Instinct 3	Death 44
Human Instincts 4	Enforcement of Rule 45
Man and Truth 6	Faith and Foresight 47
God in Conscience 8	Retribution 49
Spiritual Prayer 12	Divine Government 50
Science of Things Outward . . 14	Collective Government . . . 52
Intuition and Verification . . 16	Faith,—Trust and Belief . . 53
Axioms of Religion 20	Special Providence 57
Functions of Unbelief . . . 21	The Material and the Moral . 59
Intellectual Deism 22	Immortality of God's Beloved . 62
Rectitude of God 24	The Infiniteness of the Finite . 64
Truthfulness of God 25	Soul and Body 67
Blessedness of God 26	Worth of the Soul 68
The Love of God 27	Animal Development 69
Sin and Holiness 29	Brotherhood of Men 73
The Letter and the Spirit . . 31	The Alternatives 75
Evil 32	Future of the Righteous . . . 77
Childish and Manly Virtue . . 33	Future of the Wicked . . . 79
The Moral and the Spiritual . 34	Prevenient Grace 81
Instruction in Virtue . . . 36	Waters of Lethe 82
Objects of Teaching 37	The Doubter 84
Self-convicted Teachers . . . 39	Historical Warnings 84
Individualism and Unity . . . 41	Modern Polytheism . . , . . 86

BOOK II.

Abstract Truth 89	Pleasure . : 101
Freedom from Error 90	Conjugal Relations . . . 102
Praise and Blame 91	Church and State . . . 104
Religion 94	The Church Internally . . 105
Virtue 95	Sacred Books 106
Social Virtue 96	Teaching and Public Prayer . 107
Justice 97	Rebuke and Prophecy . . . 108
The Passions 98	Education 109
Happiness 99	Short Creeds 111
Utilitarianism 100	

BOOK III.

	PAGE.		PAGE.
CALL TO GOD'S SERVICE	113	POLITICAL EXPEDIENCY	143
POSTURES OF DEVOTION	114	POLITICAL VACILLATION	145
JOY AND CONSOLATION	116	THE ORDER OF PROGRESS	147
DESPONDENCY OF PROVIDENCE	117	VITALITY OF SIN	149
MODERN MARTYRDOM	118	STRENGTH OUT OF WEAKNESS	151
PERFECT AND IMPERFECT VIRTUES	121	LAWFUL OBEDIENCE	152
MORAL CONTAGION	124	DEFENSIVE WAR	154
FOUNDATION OF THE STATE	125	MILITARY OATHS	155
LOYALTY AND ALLEGIANCE	127	THE HARDENED POLITICIAN	157
PATRIOTISM	128	THE CONSIDERATE POLITICIAN	158
STATE PUNISHMENTS	130	TRUTH	158
PREVENTION OF CRIME	133	OATHS AND SOLEMN AFFIRMATIONS	161
MURDER	134	CLEANLINESS	162
THE TWO-FOLD LAW	138	FOOD AND DRINK	165
POMPS AND VANITIES	140	RIGHTS OF ANIMALS	167
LUXURY	141	ADORATION	170
THE ELECT	142	EPILOGUS	172

THEISM,

DOCTRINAL AND PRACTICAL.

PROLOGUS.

VIRTUE is Man's highest good,
Justice the chief virtue between man and man.
Truth makes sure the instincts of Virtue;
Free Thought is needed for the search of Truth.

Man has a mind for Virtue and Truth,
As truly as limbs for useful Labour,
And Labour and Virtue are close akin.
Labour of head or Labour of hand
Are needful to health of mind and body.
Either Labour is noble and right;
No rightful Labour ought to be debasing.

Freedom to be virtuous is for ever man's right;
And whatever or whoever forbids it, is vicious.
Never can Society be propped by Vice,
For all Vice is weakness and rottenness.
Civilization must breed noble citizens:
Degraded classes never build it up,
But always undermine and ruin it.
Degradation is unnatural, and therefore unnecessary.

Man's higher Instinct leads to lofty aspiration,
To generous sentiment and boundless desire,
Till he seeks and finds the Author of his Soul.
In seeking for him he promotes his virtue,

By finding him he is made strong within,
And being strong he strengthens his brethren.
For to aid the weak is the duty of the strong,
And thus Virtue within becomes Justice without.

Women are weakest and women most need defence,
Yet in Christian cities they are trampled under foot,
Through the league between Mammon and spurious Policy.
Nor do Time and Progress in wealth and science
Lessen or soften the hideous curse;
For no one attempts to *prevent* or *punish*,
While souls and bodies are trafficked in.

When Woman is duly honoured and homes are purified,
And Fiery Drink is withheld from the weak in mind,
And the traffickers in Sin are pursued as Felons,
And Truth is open-mouthed, and Thought is Free;
God shall soon bless the land with blessings undreamed of.
Labour shall be honoured and enmity of classes cease,
Poverty shall be light-hearted, Pauperism shall wane,
Beggary and Roguery shall be trades extinct,
The jails and the houses of the Insane shall be idle,
Health shall be robuster and Orphanhood rare,
Orphans shall meet new love in families,
Youth shall be reared to pure thought, pure fancy,
High hope, high desire and tender piety.
Religion shall grow wise and Knowledge religious,
Atheism shall waste away, and Selfishness learn to blush,
And God shall be our God and we will be his people.

FIRST BOOK.

THE THEORY OF RELIGION.

ANIMAL INSTINCT.

To know thoroughly the passions and emotions of animals,
Is a study vast and various to the learned naturalist.
Yet even the common mind and the untutored savage
In every age and land discerns and marvels at Instinct;
Observes the clever beaver, the provident ant and bee,
Maternal affections and maternal solicitudes.

Closer observation everywhere shows to the more thoughtful,
That a wisdom higher than the animal's guides the animal.
The hen who sits upon eggs to hatch her chickens,
Sits also on strange eggs or on eggs of chalk;
Nor will any one assert that in her silly brain
Is knowledge to foresee the issue of her long patience.—

That the instinct is blind, by which brutes are multiplied,
And that the parents have no longings for a noble posterity,
Perhaps no one hitherto, sane or insane, has questioned.—
The geometry is celebrated, which constructs the honeycell,
Husbanding the wax with scientific thrift,
Yet none imagine that the bee is mentally a geometer:
Nor, when the salmon of the briny sea, untaught by parents,
Struggle up sweet torrents and leap the lashers,
Will it be thought that they know the true purposes of their pilgrimage.

In these and in very many other instincts of animals
Mankind discerns a Mind higher than of the animal,
Which plans and decrees, and orders a beautiful world;
A Mind assuredly not lodged in the narrow animal brain,
Nor born with its organs, nor decaying with its death;
A Mind, visible as directly as each man's mind to his fellow,

Yet not restricted to the limits of a visible body,
Nor otherwise dependent on any known organism.
   So false is the assertion strangely current with some men,
That "*Experience* shows us mind nowhere except in Brains."
Contrariwise, Experience of every animal existence
Displays abundantly on all sides Mind that urges the brute,
Exterior, older, higher and overruling.
   That this Mind is *moral*, is not clear from the instincts of brutes;
And those who study these alone, might rest as Pantheists,
Discerning a World-Spirit, mighty, wise and provident,
Yet not ascribing to him approval of human virtue.
But Atheism which denies all higher mind whatsoever,
And pretends that Thought is limited to tangible organs,
Starts from arbitrary falsehood, and has no standing ground.
   Man's lower instincts, equally as those of brutes,
Even when unchecked by man's wisdom, are subject to a higher wisdom,
Which overrules ferocity, ambition and pride,
As in the wars of savages, heartless as wolves or lions.
Yet out of fierceness rises the dominion of Energy,
And the most energetic tribes are otherwise the noblest:
Thus the noblest bear rule, and mankind is advanced,
Even before Conscience has ripened to guide them to a better way.
And in the infancy of self-consciousness, man dimly sees God,
A God of wisdom and of energy, a God of war,
Nor can Atheism ever take root in the intellect, though barbaric:
So plain and so striking are the proofs of superior Mind,
And of the Power which guides and rules, as Lord of life.

HUMAN INSTINCTS.

   Wild men yield themselves to the guidance of instinct,
And gratify impulse as they have might and means.
Then instinct fights against instinct and force against force,
Until self-restraint is imposed by necessity and by shame:
And from suffering rises wisdom, which puts forth novel precepts,
And separates the instincts into baser, nobler, and noblest,
And honours the higher, and sets limits for the lower.
Then profligates are punished, and patriot warriors are praised,

And the sage and the artizan have their several meed of esteem.
    False prophets haply arise then, to teach abnormal follies,
As though man, by ceasing to be man, could come nearer to God,
And earn the favour of the Highest by sacrificing nature.
But the stoutest souls of mankind and the loftiest minds everywhere
Scorn to be crippled and mutilated as victims for God's altar;
And know that what is meaner, or is meanest, or is highest,
Has each its place in the world, rightful and needful:
Nor can the actions or emotions of religion ever claim a whole life.
To feed himself and aid his fellows is man's first task:
He is a citizen before he is a saint, and a citizen he remains alway.
    But afterward come philosophers, who study the world of matter,
Who are wise about the body and its influences on the mind,
Who are skilled in science and in knowledge multifarious,
And from honest love of truth long to explode delusion.
When they find the nations beguiled by a hundred superstitions,
They pity men's ignorance; and to cure our follies, they say:
"Listen not to priests, who forbid the pious to marry,
Who make merit of fasting, who bid you to renounce vanities,
Who haply allure you to a cloistered conventual life;
Who talk against riches, and against enjoyment of ear and eye;
As though the senses were impure, and affection blamable,
The indulgence of taste a weakness, and comfort ignominious.
Whatever enjoyment is lawful, enjoy ye with a good conscience:
Whatever brings you most pleasure, seek for it, if it harm not your neighbour.
Of *one* instinct only take heed and beware ye,—for it is dangerous,—
The instinct of *religion*, which seeks after God.
Cripple it, crush it, tear it out by the roots;
For from it have come wars and controversies and exclusions
And heartburnings endless; but *Truth* it will never reach."
    Instinct is but a dumb pointer; this know we very well:
It cannot guide reasonings, nor frame thought into sentences,
Nor interpret its own movements, nor verify its suggestions:
The work of establishing *Truth* falls alway to the Intellect.
But take away the instincts, and man has no desire,
No passion, no devotion, no approvals and no will.
No material can remain to be carved into moral science,
Sharp tool as the mind may be, if moral instinct be destroyed.
And the instinct of Religion is the noblest of them all,
The bravest, the most enduring, the most fruitful in mighty deeds,
The source of earliest grandeur, unitress of scattered tribes;

Even in the crudeness of its infancy, when unpurified by Science,
Yet teeming with civilization, with statesmanship, with letters,
Mistress of all high art, and parent of glorious martyrs.
And if from it have come wars and bigotries and cruelties,
Through infantine hot-headedness and unripeness of the mind,
We take your aid, O sceptics! to purge it from all such evils,
And kindly honour we pay to you for your battles against superstition:
Yet the very evils ye deplore, prove Religion's mighty energy
And the grasp deeply seated which she has within human hearts.
Nor may we esteem your philosophy, when you uphold the *lower* instincts,
And praise tasteful enjoyment, and all the pleasures of sense,
And the sweetness of human love, and the ease of wealth and luxury;
Yet are fain to blot out and quench the *highest* instinct of man,
Life to his purest morals, feeder of his noblest hopes,
Fountain of his deepest joy, and centre of his richest love.

MAN AND TRUTH.

The sage of Athens who first made Morals a philosophy,
Had abandoned in despair the ungrateful study of Physics;
Because students on opposite sides taught things incongruous,
Being related, one to another, as madman to madman.
For, some thought the Universe to be single, others that it was infinite in number;
Some, that everything was in motion; others, that motion was impossible;
Birth and Death seemed to some to go on always, to others never.
Socrates therefore wondered, that to the thoughtful it was not manifest,
How impossible it is to man to attain Truth in Physics.
But what things are moral, what the Gods have purposed and approve,
On *this* he judged that a wise man should bestow his study.

Some philosophers of modern times would reverse his doctrine.
They abandon in despair the ungrateful study of Religion;
Because students on opposite sides teach things incongruous,
Being related, one to another, as madman to madman.
For, some think the Church to be single, others that it is infinite in number;
Some, that the Pope is infallible, others that infallibility is impossible;
Miracles seem to some to go on in every age, to others never.
These philosophers therefore wonder, that to the thoughtful it is not manifest,
How impossible it is to man to attain Truth in Religion.

But what things are tangible, measurable, ponderable, computable,
On *this* they judge that a wise man should bestow his study.

   Both the one and the other enact arbitrary exclusion,
If the same God made the outer world and made the human heart.
He who studies the forces of Planets, studies a force of God;
And he who studies the energies of Conscience, studies an energy of God.
Each is a Divine study, each is a Theology.
All knowledge is partial, and ignorance is everywhere infinite:
If man cannot know God wholly, neither can he wholly know himself.
Complete knowledge is not given to us, but partial knowledge is given,
Alike in Physics and in Morals and in the spiritualism of Theology;
Such knowledge as suffices for life and godliness.
For, moral law is a revealing of inward sentiment,
And God's moral laws are legible both in each heart and in mankind;
And when one knows another's sentiments and powers and ways,
He knows him enough both for confidence and for love.

   If Galileo and Kepler had desponded of Truth with Socrates,
Never would they have laid the foundations of modern Physics.
But they had *faith* that man's mind was made to attain Truth,
And that the Universe was fitly propounded to his study;
Else never would their patience and zeal have lasted out.
So too, if any one despond of Religious truth,
He enfeebles his own efforts, and is little likely to attain it.
Indeed such despondency is irrational *now*,
When Astronomy and Geology have achieved such conquests.—
"Oh God! I think thy thoughts after thee!"
Said Kepler, on getting a small glimpse of a vast theory.
But now that so many of "God's thoughts" are revealed
Through ages long past and in the distant heavens,
Beyond Arcturus, beyond the Pleiades,
Before man's birth, and before the mountains were reared;
Who shall think man's mind uncognizant of God's laws?
Faith in the harmony of Earth and Heaven has opened Nature,
Faith in the same harmony is the key to Religion.

   If the laws of Mechanics which rule on Earth ruled not in Heaven,
Never could physical astronomy have taken its first step,
Nor Newton have revealed Heaven's laws by genius.
And if the laws of Goodness ruling within Man ruled not in Heaven,
Never could moral theology take a single step,
Nor could genius be inspired, nor revelation have value.
But if the law of the Conscience is God's command to virtue,

Then the *same* law of Goodness rules in Heaven and in Earth;
And by the study of Goodness we learn the mind of God,
As from action on Earth's surface we learn the Mechanics of Heaven.
   Light is natural to the Eye, and the Eye improves under Light,
So Truth is natural to the Mind, and the Mind improves under Truth.
But the student of Goodness must himself become good,
So far at least as to choose Goodness for his best portion.
If base passion or worldliness is allowed to domineer,
No man can gaze steadily at Purity and at God.
And then perhaps he despairs of religious truth,
And moralizes on man's feebleness and limited faculties,
So unfitted to fathom the Divine and to know the Eternal!
   He who would watch the stars, the planets and their satellites,
Must keep his instruments in good state and use them to advantage,
And must interpret their indications with sound good sense,
With a mind mature and simple, unpreoccupied by superstition.
And he who would study the morals and government of God,
Must purify his conscience and apply it wisely, -
And must interpret its indications with sound good sense,
With a mind mature and simple, unpreoccupied by superstition.
The pure in heart will always know something of God,
But from the perfection of the whole mind is the unveiling of religious certainties.

GOD IN CONSCIENCE.

   In the Sun and Moon and Stars is an ever-acting energy,
In the Tides and in the Sea Currents and in the running Rivers,
In the Clouds, in the Oceanic Winds, in the Frost and Hail,
In the leaves and buds of the Forest, in the Grasses and in the Seaweed.
This energy is visible to savage and sage, confessed by all:
Atheists call it a Law and Life, Theists hold it to be divine.
   There is likewise an energy and active life in every animal,
From oyster and starfish to whale and dog and man,
A vegetative principle in the Animal as truly as in the Tree.
That force in the animal stomach which brews the juices,
That force in the lungs which blends the air with the blood,
Is vegetative and chemical, as the forces in the leaves of the tree,
Nor can the will of the animal increase or arrest the force.

This energy of life within is *ours*, yet it is not *we*:
It is in us, it belongs to us, yet we cannot control it.
It acts without bidding, even when we do not think of it,
Nor will it cease acting at our command, or otherwise obey us.
Atheists call it a Law and a Life, but say that "it is not a Mind;
"It is a brute movement of Nature, a *blind* eternal force:"
Yet they admit that it exists, and that it is prepotent,
And is a law or force pervading the Universe.

   They farther admit, and indeed maintain, and warn us,
That man is apt to conflict with this force within him,
A force eternal, irresistible, certain to defeat him.
Namely, if he practise that which the Law of his health forbids,
The Law will take its vengeance and will despoil him of health,
And he is utterly helpless against the overmastering might.
It is *in* him, but not *of* him; he is subject to it.
The Atheist adds: "It is *blind*, not intelligent or moral."

   But not against the powers of the bodily life only do men fight;
Often also we call into conflict an inward moral power.
For when we are tempted to sin and follow inclination to evil,
A voice within forbids, and summons us to refrain;
And if we bid it to be silent, it yet is not still; it is not in our control.
It acts without our order, without our asking, against our will.
It is *in* us, it belongs to us, but it is not *of* us; it is *above* us.
Perseverance in evil may deaden our ear or stifle that voice,
If indeed there is wickedness to which Conscience never speaks:
But *while* it recalls from evil, and reproaches us for evil,
And is not silenced by our effort, surely it is not *we*:
Yet it is a moral force, such as pervades all moral minds,
Being in you, as it is in me, and as it was in men deceased.

   But of what kind is this force, within us, and not in our control?
Will the Atheist say, "It is *blind*, not intelligent or moral?"
This would be absurd, opposed to the manifest reality:
For it is both intelligent and moral, and higher than our sinning will.
Nay, and whosoever defies this inward monitor,
He first suffers pain while fighting an unnatural battle;
As when one endures the pains of bodily disorder.
But next, as disease becomes inveterate and no longer acute,
And organs degenerate, and health is permanently marred;
So the man, who has fought against the higher inward law,
At length becomes callous and his moral organs are debased,
And his moral health is gone, and the Law takes its revenge.

This energy of the Conscience is *in* us, *above* us, and not *of* us,
It is moral, it is intelligent, it is not *we*, nor at our bidding ;
It pervades mankind, as one Life pervades the trees ;
It is mighty, it is commanding : and *what* then is it ?
Let it not be called *arbitrary*, when the Theist replies :
" The Life which is in all Nature is the Life within every Conscience,*
" Intelligent, Moral, Mighty, and our natural Lord."
 Nay ; arbitrary it is not, but rightfully concluded.
The Power to which we ascribe these actions within the Conscience,
Is already known to exist, and to be a Designing Mind,
Seen to us most distinctly in the instincts of animals.
The idea of such a Mind is not suggested first from Conscience,
Is not a " Hypothesis " imagined to account for the phenomena ;
But its existence was discovered before the Conscience was studied,
Discerned as a *fact*, equally with the minds of other men.
We descry also its action in all the fitnesses of Nature,
The fitness of the Eye for Light, of Night for Sleep,
With ten thousand other marks of Wisdom and Design.
But this Power, though known to exist, was known imperfectly,
Nor may we ever say that we know *all* its attributes.
Previously we discovered its mightiness and ruling forethought ;
And now we farther discover its moral will,
As commanding the Right and forbidding us from the Wrong.
The *moral* nature of God is made sure to us from Conscience alone.
 Contemplate further, that when we have descried a superior Mind
Inspiring and guiding the unconscious Bee and Swallow,
A Mind that dictates and governs through regions unlimited ;
It were strange indeed, if this ruling Power so thoughtful
Confined its cares and commands to the lower animals.
Nay, but if it inspire maternal cares in the Hen,
The same mind inspires maternal love in the Woman.
And all would expect, even *before* studying Conscience,
That a Power which overrules all the lower instincts,
Must exert some rule also amid the higher,
And act upon Conscience, if it act for Maternal Love.
Thus *beforehand* the thing is to be expected by good sense,
And *afterward* observation exhibits it in fact ;
Whereby the argument answers the severest claims of Science.

---

* This form of the argument is taken from a review of Theodore Parker on Atheism, etc., which appeared in the 'Inquirer' (London Newspaper) of Nov. 12th, 1853, and is attributed to the pen of Mr. Richard Hutton.

Nor need any one wonder, that, whereas men of every age
Have believed in the activity of superior Mind,—
A belief characteristic of the human species,—
So too the wisest have always, in some measure and degree,
Ascribed to that Mind a moral will and rule.
For, God has not left himself unrevealed to man;
And it is no newly invented doctrine, but old and widely spread,
That Conscience is to man a voice of God within.

Yet those who have thus taught, (and taught, we see, cogently,)
Never intended to impute to the Conscience infallibility.
Let none imagine that we hold a notion so untenable,
Refuted by facts too numerous and obvious to need mention.
But if the Atheist, avowing that he ill understands the Conscience,
Urge its weakness as inconsistent with our notion of the Divine,
Let him remark, that in truth we are nowise inconsistent,
Who hold life and instinct and conscience to be energies of God,
Alike finite, alike imperfect, alike liable to be choked,
To be weakened or strengthened, or to be in some sense perverted.
The physical life over which we have no control, and which is not we,
Is an energy of God, say we; but we say not, it is perfect God;
None attributes to it omnipotence or other divine perfections.
Nor, the more, does any attribute to conscience divine infallibility.
The two cases are alike, and this has no more difficulty than that:
For the same reason, ancient men spoke of God's *Spirit*,
As something short of God himself; as we say *Energy* and *Influence*.

Remember also, that close observers have often moralized
On the tender conscience of youth, uncorrupted as yet by the world.
The Experience of life, on which some would found morality,
In no respect tends to communicate the love of goodness,
Generosity, self-sacrifice or other high enthusiasm.
These spiritual powers, and all quick discernment of nobleness,
Seem to be born in the soul from God and brought into the world,
And there far oftener to be deadened than quickened.
Experience informs us what results will come from certain actions,
(Which is not always known beforehand) and explains many details;
And thus it is necessary, equally with right impulse, for sound judgment,
Yet it cannot of itself give right impulse nor right choice.
Much rather from solitude, from meditation on scenes of beauty,
From adoration of that God whom we recognise as the Power in Conscience,
Than from any observation of the world, is the heart made moral;
Or if it be strongly moved by teaching and by sympathy,

It is not by *that* teaching which talks of worldly Experience and Happiness:
It is the voice of the spiritual teacher, who believes in God,
And avows him our inward judge, searching the heart,
That awakens the dull conscience to a sounder morality.
Thus is the doctrine of "God in the Conscience" suitably confirmed.

SPIRITUAL PRAYER.

From the earliest day when Hebrew Psalmists breathed spiritual longings,
(And perhaps much earlier, if Eastern documents were extant,)
It is visible that pious men believed God to answer prayer.
And when so many thousands, from age to age,
In various nations, account prayer to be a spiritual power,
We seem to have their joint attestation of its efficacy,
A valid proof which may be accepted by reasonable bystanders.
   Yet this attestation loses weight with thoughtful minds
Who together with dogmas have dropt the use of Prayer,
And who dread to be fanatical if they yield to inward Instinct;
It loses weight with them, I say, because the public voice of Churches
Raises petition to the most High for manifold outward good;
Such petition as cannot without miracle be granted,
Or such as makes the common Father a partizan in human strife.
When they see that devotees century after century go on,
Lifting up prayers which undoubtedly receive no reply,
Yet discover not their misplaced toil and their futile hopes;
Then the philosopher undervalues the attestations of the religious,
If they aver that God strengthens them in reply to spiritual prayer;
But he holds that the worshipper, heated by excitement, deludes himself,
And, having acted on his own heart, supposes that God has acted on it.
   Nor is it easy to give to such men attestations,
Which, as in other science, they must accept as "experimental proof."
For they cannot themselves make the experiment,
Since they have not the Faith, without which the experiment is void.
Nor can they enter the heart of others who pray,
And take scientific precautions lest the experiment be delusive;
And measure what was the moral strength *before* the prayer,
And what accession of strength has come *after* the prayer.
Nay, and what is more, those prayers which are printed for all men,

By their very universality least touch the sore places of individuals;
And the prayers which are most fervent, deepdrawn and effective,
Are those which each shelters in the recesses of his soul,
And seldom could lay open, even to him or her who is dearest,
Without harm to the simplicity and truthfulness of prayer:
So sacred and so secret is the prayer which is best answered.
Yet this very thing is by the reasoner called Excitement,
And he distrusts the man's judgment of such deep inward facts.
  Natural and innocent instinct brings with it its own warrant.
In the agony of fear or of sorrow Prayer *will* burst forth,
And even if it ask amiss, it yet may have its uses,
Bearing perhaps fruit within which was not asked for.
Much more the prayer which asks inward conformity to God's mind
Is fully justified to every man by direct Intuition,
When, pressed by spiritual instinct, he unloads his heart
And pours out complaint, sorrow, desire and hope
To the ear and into the bosom of the Invisible Potentate.
Such prayers need no argument and no apology:
Yet neither do they always accompany the highest spiritual state.
Thanksgiving and Adoration are well called *the Breath of the Soul*,
Which in man or angel show the acting of spiritual life.
But could we be perfect, we should need no personal Prayer,
Nor is Prayer equally needed at all times and by all men.
Still, each one who knows its value must needs wish to recommend it,
And to remove, if possible, the objections of the oversubtle.
Let us then calmly assay to prove this matter as a THEOREM.
  We start with assuming what already has been proved,
That the Conscience above us is an Energy of God within,
Who acts on the soul through the soul, unbidden,
Just as his vegetative power, unbidden, acts in the body.
He who prays for spiritual strength prays not solely to a God without,
In the stars and in the sun and in the wide ocean,
But to the God whom he discerns speaking to him by conscience,
In him and yet not of him, a superior force.
And as he who fights against conscience resists God within;
So he who lays low his heart in prayer surrenders to God,
And, so far as man's will reaches, he casts down the obstacles,
Which are a screen against the rays of the divine glory;
Not otherwise, than as when one who is dark within his house
Throws open his shutters to admit the light of the sun.
Then by his own proper act he has light and warmth not his own,

Poured out from a foreign source, from the luminary in heaven.
So the man who has opened the window of his heart to God,
(To that God who is in his conscience,) does *naturally* receive God's rays.
And if by mere self-surrender his prayer attains its end,
As, the vanquishing of a temptation or the enlivening of a virtue,
(Which the philosopher thus resolves into a purely human process,)
Even so, no one who believes at all in an inward spiritual God
Can hesitate to affirm that *God has answered his prayer*.

But we contend not for words and for empty phraseology.
Call it Conscience or call it God; if others can perform the same act
And win the same blessing, it is so far not amiss.
But if by calling it *mere Conscience* they fall out of both prayer and blessing,
Let us not seem obtrusive in grieving at the loss.

One step more must we take, and an important one.
"Prayer does not only yield to a force *already* within,
"But draws into us therewith a *strengthening* of that force."
For if it be admitted that God dwells naturally in the Conscience
And acts on the human spirit by normal natural energy,
As normal and as natural as the other powers of nature,
But moral and spiritual, not a mere blind force;
While we know that this energy is not naturally constant,
But varies both from man to man, and in the same man from time to time,
And is repressed by obstinate sin and often becomes *weaker:*
Dry Reason would expect that to obedience it would grow *stronger*.
Who then,—having faith that God is the fountain of Holiness
And approves of our virtue and enjoins its advancement,—
Can doubt, that when we pray and surrender our Worse,
Not only thereby do we welcome the Better that *was* within,
But the living Source of that Better swells the flood of his presence,
So that the Conscience itself becomes sounder and purer and stronger,
Broadening, deepening, enlivening the inward moral forces?

SCIENCE OF THINGS OUTWARD.

Two opposite views are often heard concerning Science,
In its aspect and relation toward God and things divine.
There are some who suppose that the Science of things outward,
Of mechanism, of chemistry, of organic and social life,
Furnishes all the substance for metaphysical and religious truth,

And by its registration and observations of Quantity
Supersedes the rude results supplied by mere consciousness.
They conceive of a Religion that shall be built up out of external facts,
Marshalled and measured by Science, and sharply defined,
And see not that such a religion remains ever outside the heart,
Having no sentiment, no self-knowledge, no spiritual access to God.

There are others (partly friends, partly foes of Science,)
Who maintain that Science is deadly to all Religion whatsoever.
And the one wish to establish Science on the ruins of Religion,
The others to fortify Religion by the demolition of Science.
But both are of accord that the two are implacable enemies,
Unable to exist side by side, much less to unite in harmony.

Of these extreme opinions hardly could either be wholly false,
Though neither is wholly true; nay, each is more false than true.
For, the Science of things outward cannot give all Religious knowledge,
Nor yet is it hostile to Religion, but surely to false Religion:
And to think soberly of this matter is of no small value.

The Science of things quantitative gives at once this vast advantage,
(Peculiarly precious for religion and for practical faith,)
An absolute confidence of the mind in the certainty of Truth,
That it is unchangeable, and cannot be tampered with.
This confidence is earned by exercise in Geometry, in Numbers,*
In every sort of Calculus, though dry and void of sentiment;
Also in Mechanics and Astronomy and all the branches of Chemistry,
And in everything called Physics and in the study of Organic Life.
Whereas those whose culture is from Poetry alone and Fine Art,
And from History and from Oratory and from practical Politics,
Are prone to believe in the universal virtue of compromise
And in the absence of fixed laws and in the anarchy of genius,
And to explode as *Platitudes* all broad moralities.
And their virtue is too superficial, based on shifting opinion
Or on partial expediency, all pliant and unrigid.
But neither Morals nor Religion can attain spiritual vigour
Without Faith in absolute Law, such as Science vehemently teaches.

Science also tears down mercilessly the strongholds of superstition,
And shatters Pagan idols and roots up magic and polytheism,
And clears off choking nuisances, and sends in the free air,
And with confidence in Law gives to men Free Thought,
And proclaims the virtue of Truth, and steels the mind to choose it,
Though it affront our old prejudices and expose us to men's ill-will.
This again is a vast service performed by Science to Religion,

Which stands by Truth alone, in love of Truth, and by Free Thought.
  Lastly, from the great sciences which deal in the Heavens and in Time,
Which scan the farness of the Stars and the age of the Earth;
And from the science of Organic Life, which spies into tiny animals
And into the fineness of vegetation, by the aid of the microscope;
We learn how measureless is God's world great and small,
And its vast duration in the ages that are past;
And imagination spreads wide to clasp ideas so mighty,
And clothes with new grandeur the Ruler of the Universe.
Yea, though his Infinity still shoots beyond imagination,
We gain thoughts less unworthy of him, more manly in growth,
And we drop childish errors, and become nobler in mind,
And our religion grows into manhood, without knowing how or why.
To the moderns have men of science thus been true prophets of God.
  So from Science comes to Religion its bony fabric and solidity,
Its simple consistent strength, its harmony and its purity,
Its grandeur and dignity, its universality.
But the science of matter cannot give knowledge of soul,
Nor teach of Free Will and of Habit, of the Conscience, and of Right,
Nor supersede all study of the mind and its actions,
Nor furnish with true sentiment, with right loves and right hatreds,
Nor investigate spiritual phenomena or spiritual laws;
And cover our bony fabric with flesh, and fill it with life.
These topics may haply be all at length grasped in one New Science,
Aided by the hints of earlier science, and following their clue:
But as Geometry cannot teach Optics, though it give good service,
So neither can all the Physical Sciences together teach Religion.
And he who, thinking himself a philosopher, studies the outer world alone,
Passing by Consciousness and Conscience, the Moral and the Spiritual,
He makes himself but a half-philosopher and does no justice to Truth.

INTUITION AND VERIFICATION.

  All Science presumes the accuracy of its informants,
Of the eye, of the ear, of the mind which dictates axioms,
Also of the mind which directs processes of reasoning:
Or the informant may be some useful tool craftily adapted,
The telescope, the barometer, the thermometer, the rain-guage,
The hygrometer, the microscope, the sextant, the theodolite.

Yet none of these is infallible, each needs to be verified;
To be tried and corrected in the advances of the Science.
Until it has been tested, its truth is but presumptive;
But after it has stood trial, its information is trustworthy,
Though it need a wise interpreter and allowance for illusions.
   But only the mind can direct the verifications,
Differing in each science and suited to the special case;
And the mind too is fallible, and itself needs to be verified,
And into many a delusion has the human mind fallen.
Thus there is wheel within wheel, error tangled in error,
And many a long birth-throe in the travail of science.
Yea, if religion has miscarried and brought forth folly,
No less has other science teemed with delusions,
With complex contradictions and with changes backward and forward;
Till manifold experience and the joint work of many nations,
Many ages, many geniuses, has slowly unfolded truth.
   Direct perception of truth may be called *Intuition*,
As though the mind *gazed* on truth, like to an eye that sees objects.
Thus are the Axioms of Geometry believed and counted certain
By mere contemplation of what they assert.
To verify the intuition and the first principles which it furnishes,
The science must first go onward to practical results;
Then we put the whole science to the test of Congruity:
Whether it harmonize with itself, and also with the real world.
If *No*, then an error must have crept in somewhere.
If *Yes*, this is by no means always cogent of truth,
(For within certain limits falsehood also may be consistent),
But it is more cogent, as the intuitions are more fruitful of result.
For if results be numerous and practical, any pervading error
Must often burst into contrariety, and will somewhere be visible.
   A *second* Harmony is found in the agreement of many minds,
When all of the students have the same first perceptions,
And acquiesce in the same reasonings, and attain the same results.
   Or sometimes the Harmony takes a special form,
Yielding a *third* verification, more peculiarly valued,
When the organ or science becomes a new Power or faculty,
As, a power of predicting what can be tested in other ways.
Thus the telescope unveils distant things dim to the eye,
And a nearer view confirms its notices.
Thus the mathematician by some short cut gives arduous results,
Which by tedious trials the learner verifies.

Thus the astronomer predicts eclipses and detects the longitude,
And the hour brings the eclipse, and clocks confirm the longitude,
Hereby the science and its processes and its tools are proved.
Knowledge takes many forms of power, familiar to us now;
As in navigation, and as in the telegraph, and in other wondrous chemistry.
   Not otherwise stand the arguments of Morality and of Religion,
So far as unlike knowledge may fall under like tests.
By direct perception, by rudimentary intuition,
Are the first notions and beliefs conveyed to mankind.
Crude may be the instinct and sometimes fallacious,
Yet growing sounder and purer with moral growth;
Advancing also in reasonable self-confidence,
Even as with scientific culture grows confidence in science.
Moreover, Harmony of results unites moral thought,
And the voice of mankind echoes fundamental Harmony,
So that in distant ages and lands, alike among the rude and the cultivated,
(Despite of false philosophy) there is a like belief in Free Will,
Like approval of the Generous, the Brave, the Truthful, the Chaste,
The Temperate, the Kindly, the Industrious, the Merciful.
All nations have these words, devised to express approval.
So too is spread abroad the belief of a Great Spirit in Nature,
A perfect Energy, a conscious Intellect, a pervading Law.
   A second verification is, from the Power of Happiness,
Which the cherishing of virtue sheds into hearts.
For, Happiness, *unaimed at** by each man to himself,
Comes in no small measure to each, as he gains inward harmony,
And to all parts of society from the improved morals of the rest.
And because the pursuit of Happiness by each would *ruin** Virtue,
Therefore the more weighty testimony is its arrival unsought.
Moral culture likewise gives Power to the man,
Making him master of himself and of his faculties, abler on all sides,
Fitter for all service and for all pursuits of high knowledge,
More valuable to other men and more independent of fortune.
Nor can we believe that this inward Power is an accident,
Or that it could accrue from a science false at bottom.
   Still higher is a like verification raised in Religion,

---

* The perfect Disinterestedness of Virtue is the main subject of the eloquent and learned "Essay on Intuitive Morals," which has appeared so seasonably, in refreshing contrast to the stifling moral heresies generally dominant. It unites the rigour of the Stoic with the seraphic fire of the Calvinist and the human sympathy of the Unitarian Christian. [By Frances Power Cobbe; — Williams and Norgate.]

Which even in its rudeness is always an intense Power,
But in its purer spiritualism becomes a Power of *Good*.
If Morals be true, Spiritual Worship cannot be vain :
For nothing so enables man to withstand temptation,
To endure calamity or to persevere in courageous virtue,
As the belief in a present God, listening to our voice,
Whose eye watches our conduct and approves our rectitude.

   This faith may at first be feeble and wavering,
As is the faith of a learner in scientific processes ;
But as the learner wins confidence in his theorems and in his formulas,
Yea, and in his own powers of reasoning, by frequent trial,
So he who strives after virtue, learning by experience
What is Religion's Power, gains confirmation to his faith ;
And the Intuitions which before were trusted, yet anxiously,
By trial are proved trustworthy, and themselves also grow clearer.
For as the sailor's eye learns by practice to evade illusions,
And his observation becomes sensitive, and his judgment sagacious,
So does the eye of the soul and its sagacity improve by culture :
And experience strengthens Faith, until Faith grows confident,
Discerning God's Goodness and Presence, as overruling and eternal.
And when Faith becomes fruitful in gratitude and love and joy,—
Products more divine than those of Science ;
Those who reap these, will not admit to their critics
That the foundations of Religion lack Positive and practical test.

   Nor would this long be denied, were not Error confused with Truth,
Error inveterate, pretentious, and reeking with crimson stains.
Bigotry and Superstition, dressed in Religion's garb,
With hideous visage, scream curses from heaven,
And spread gloom over the history and over the destinies of man,
And revile Conscience, which is God's sacred seat,
And with presumptuous threats invade the place of God,
And thrust up individual man into unseemly eminence,
And domineer over fellow-men, as judges over culprits,
Trampling on Justice and Equity and Modesty.
Such Bigotry and Superstition cleave even to the pious,
Eating often to the heart of Religion and marring its loveliness.
These evils must be cast away, that Religion may be glorified,
That God may be fitly worshipped, and man may be blessed.

AXIOMS OF RELIGION.

To reckon up the Axioms and Postulates of Religion,
Involves no other doubt than in all the Deductive Sciences,
As in Geometry or Mechanics, where controversies still linger.
Whether Axioms be two or ten, the Science is not the less stable,
So that only every Axiom be surely affirmed by good sense.
Yet, for the beauty of reasoning, let Axioms be few,
And for its clearness, let them be simple, and in some sense co-ordinate.
Until better be proposed, we may rest in the following Axioms:
  I. "That Omnipresent Law and that Power,
      Which we discern to animate the universe, is not blind, but is intelligent."
Also, by *Definition*, we entitle this Power GOD.
  II. "The Power upon whose energy the human spirit depends,
      Must have all that spirit's faculties, and more beside."
  III. "God is observant of the moral action of man,
      And, approving our efforts for Right, disapproves our Wrong."
  IV. "The God who approves our Rectitude, is himself Perfect in Rectitude."
  V. "Adoration of God is intrinsically suitable to man."
—*Coroll*. Such Adoration therefore is pleasing to God.

Nothing would I call an Axiom, save that which Intuition furnishes,
So that thoughtful men believe it by the evidence of thought itself,
Not by conscious experience and by external proof,
Even though experiment and test from without be possible and useful.
Of such a kind, as it seems, are the Axioms here proposed,
To which most men will assent for their intrinsic reasonableness,
As to those which concern Space and Surfaces and Lines.
Nor do any of them involve language doubtful or dark,
Nor is their *assertion* arbitrary or mysterious, more than their *denial*.
They are denied by very few; and most of the rejectors
Reject them only in hatred of Bigotry and Superstition,
Which Atheists, not unnaturally, confound with Religion.
Yet to meet the denial, it is fitting to enquire for proof,
Other than that best witness which true religion brings after it.
The argument from Animal Instinct demonstrates the first Axiom:
And the arguments which show "God in the Conscience,"
Suffice to establish the second and third.
No one who believes the three first will dispute the fourth and fifth.
  On these Axioms depends the *Absolute* religion
Which belongs to every Moral being, and therefore to man.
But for *Human* and practical religion we need also a POSTULATE,

Separate in nature from those which we rank as Axioms:
—" God gives, to those who pray to him, increase of spiritual strength."
Scarcely may one say of this, that Intuition affirms the truth;
But *Instinct* prompts the act, and *Experience* affirms the truth;
Such truths are Experimental, like the " Laws " in Mechanics.
And yet by pure reasonings, without the distant experience,
This truth may be deduced from a simpler truth of experience,
Which all ages and nations everywhere attest,—
That " God within Man's Conscience commands and forbids."
Therefore, to meet secret doubts and misgivings,
The Postulate was above presented as a Theorem.

FUNCTIONS OF UNBELIEF.

  Man individually is imperfect, and Society collectively is imperfect,
Yet collective Society is less imperfect than individual man.
For, the excess of one corrects the defect of another,
When all co-operate in a common effort:
So, in the pursuit of Truth, opposite natures do good service.
The cold and the cautious, the habitually incredulous,
If they are morally sound, contribute eminently to truth,
Making progress often slower, yet being as ballast to a ship:
Nor may believers rightly look on unbelievers as enemies,
But should regard them as true friends, if their heart and eye be single.
Much benefit to India might a flood of Atheism have wrought.
In Europe, by long time and by the establishment of science,
The gulf between Belief and Unbelief perpetually lessens,
Giving hope, that as Bigotry vanishes and Love strengthens,
All shall blend in one Faith, in Religion as in other Science.
  The Paganism of Greece was believed not by the vulgar only,
But substantially also by many of the grandest intellects,
As by Homer and Æschylus, by Pindar and Sophocles,
Who may have rejected parts, yet received the whole.
Even the noblest of the Stoics, with patriotic obstinacy,
Clung to the national creed, and vainly aimed to spiritualize it.
Against this extravagant and puerile mythology
Unbelief rallied its forces in the school of Epicurus,
Who, in name admitting gods, in fact denied them functions
Or action or power, and wrought Atheism into system.

Wide indeed was the gap between that religion and its opponent.
The one taught Divine Caprice, the other Blind Chance.
Each exposed the other's errors, to the benefit of the unbiassed:
Hence both Theists and Atheists are now made wiser.
The Theist disowns all *caprice* in the Creator and Ruler,
Believes in his impartial Wisdom, and discerns that it has *Laws*.
The Atheist admits that Chance is never a cause of things,
And that the harmony of the universe is a product of Law.
Thus the contest is narrowed, and we can scan it more distinctly.
That the universe is pervaded by Forces which obey fixed Laws,
And that by such Forces the whole is enlivened and guided,
All are agreed; and that these Forces have organic harmony.
But Anti-Theists deny that this harmony implies
Unity in a Divine Mind, a Spirit, a Person.
Keen obstinate opponents undermine in us whatever is rotten,
Though never can they overthrow the solid and the true.
Fretted by men's bigotry, they are so eager to refute it,
As to be blind to the higher Wisdom which is behind Animal Instinct
And ordains the relations of the inner and the outer being:
Yet some* of them already acknowledge that Moral Laws,
Higher than man, ruling over man, pervade the human world.
When they have admitted this, they have left Atheistic ground.
Atheism has ever stood, only as a counterpoise to error,
And will vanish, when through our wisdom its function is superfluous.
Atheists are not without God, though they know him not.
When they aim sincerely after Truth, having a love of Virtue,
His Spirit is striving within them, and will not be wholly vain.

INTELLECTUAL DEISM.

Said wise men among the Greeks, "God is Intellect;
God has no passions nor emotions nor desires,
Nor loves nor hatreds, nor sentiment moral or immoral;
But he abides apart in his infinitude, solitary and eternal,
Responding not to man's affections, and deaf to his cry."

---

* "I for one have more faith in the order and harmony of Nature than in the justice or wisdom of men; and am rejoiced that it is not left to the latter to arrange the politics of the ethical world at their will."—Lionel H. Holdreth [a professed Atheist] in 'The Reasoner,' July 29th, 1857.

INTELLECTUAL DEISM.

Yet men as wise, or the very same men, said also, and said justly:
"Pure Intellect is the author of no deed whatsoever."
Intellect reveals truth or possibility, but affords no spur to action:
It spreads light over the outer scene, but the light does not kindle.
If God had no loves and no desires, he could neither be a Creator
Nor an Architect nor a Governor; but must act without Will, if at all.
Pure Intellect has no will, no desire of constructions,
No approval of Right, no living Force nor Motive.
He who believes Intellect to be Creative, believes it to be full of Aims,
Full of Desires, full of Approvals, and a student of the Good.
Precisely such we otherwise know God to be,
When we discern that it is he who speaks to us by Conscience.
His sentiments are moral, for he commands our morality:
Nor does the Infinite One abide apart, but dwells in our bosoms,
Exciting man's affections and awaiting his cry.

To assign to the most High the weak passions of struggling natures,
The anger and the impulse, caprices and partialities,
Was the error of early thought, which mature reason explodes.
Nor ascribe we to his greatness the virtues of our feebleness:
But *that* GOODNESS only, which fitly increases with Strength,
That Purity of broad Love, which suits to the tranquil and serene.
Not other can the Intellect be which has created moral man,
And the Wisdom of his Goodness is the glory, before which man must worship.

Modern Anti-Theists have adopted, as a scourge to Theists,
The Greek epithet Anthropomorphous, to frighten by its vagueness,
Which strictly means, God, *in the shape of man.*
Surely none but barbarians ascribe to God a human form,
Nor any human organs, though we speak of them by metaphor;
Necessarily: for man's speech is formed from objects of sense.
But to stigmatize by a mean epithet, used improperly,
Our learning of God through Man, is weak and unworthy.
Let men deny if they choose, that man has any Creator,
Or that there is any universal Spirit full of Intelligence:
But let them not pretend that such a Spirit does not comprise ours,
And is destitute of the elements which in us are highest.
Or if unawares we ascribe weakness to him,
Let them point out the error, and call us back to reason.
But to forbid us to infer the divine Faculties and Sentiments
By studying the human, cautiously and thoughtfully,
Can be justified by nothing but pure Atheism outright.
Such Anti-Theism is but Atheism veiled in poetry,

And if it affect to revere a God, is worse than Atheism;
For it leads straight to the rudest Paganism by deifying brute Force.
Our knowledge of Goodness is prior to our knowledge of God.
Our reverence for Goodness is prior to our reverence of God.
Fitting is it to love and revere goodness in an Atheist,
But monstrous to worship a God in whom is no Goodness.

RECTITUDE OF GOD.

The man who is in the way to improve his moral state,
(And none else is in moral health,) aspires to be better than he is,
And looks up to a higher rule, which he has not yet reached,
A nobler *ideal* of goodness, vaguely grasped by his imagination.
Whosoever has attained the virtue to which I do but look up,
Him must I needs either honour or revere.
And such is my nature, that I can revere *him* only,
In whom those virtues are *real* which are *ideal* with me.

If I believe that man or angel has reached such excellence
As my conscience approves, and such as I desire in vain;
I may honour him with a reverence increasing ever,
As the goodness rises with which my convictions clothe him.
And when I believe that God possesses Goodness *Absolute*,—
The very qualities which my conscience approves admiringly,—
Then the Veneration, mounting higher, subdues the heart
Into adoring prostration before Infinite Goodness.
This is the only adoration possible to man,
The only homage which it befits the Highest to accept:
Namely, when the heart of man sincerely believes
That the virtue, which is *ideal* in its inmost aspirations and love,
Is in the heart of God *real*, eternal, universal, incessant in action.

But if any teacher tell us that God ought to be *called* Good,
(As an honour to his wisdom, and compliment to his greatness,)
Though God have nothing in his heart that we mean by *goodness*,
Nor kindness nor justice, nor moral sentiment at all;
If we believe such a teacher, then by the necessity of our nature
We are disabled from adoring, and from rational moral homage.
We may bow down, awed by greatness, astounded by wisdom,
Or unmanned with terror; but smitten in heart to stone.
This may be called worship, but it is not loving reverence:

Conscience does not bid us revere, nor can we love such a God.
   CONSCIENCE is God within us, and unveils the God without us,
Speaking not always clearly, yet with a voice that must not be defied.
It is not the Atheist here, but the Pagan who opposes us.
For the Atheist will admit, that *if* the Life in Nature be intelligent
And designed man's goodness, it must itself be Good,
Nor could anything warp the most High from perfect Rectitude.
But the Pagan pretends that the Cleverness and Power beyond us
Is reckless of our morality and justly shocks our Conscience,
Yet deserves from us homage and adoration and praise.
But if Conscience cannot approve him, Conscience forbids to praise him.
Even Gratitude is painful, if we disesteem our benefactor,
And to have needed his favours seems like a calamity.
The worship of such an one is from Fear, not from Morality and Duty:
The religion is devil-worship, depraving and debasing,
Vile and immoral, as the worship of a Venus or of a Moloch.
   But with thoughtful men this fable is long exploded,
And that *there is no God but a good God* is a chief certainty of all admissible religion.
The night of Paganism is gone: light from Jerusalem has dawned,
Though degenerate Christians may strive to quell it.
" Be ye holy, for I am holy,"——was God's precept according to the Levites :
." We will aspire toward thy holiness," shall the heart of mankind respond.

TRUTHFULNESS OF GOD.

   The truthfulness of God is comprised in his Rectitude,
Nor can any cultivated mind for a moment question it;
Yet a few words on this head may be not ill-bestowed.—
There are persons, not the thoughtless only, but some of the educated,
Who marvellously blunder here as to the source of our knowledge,
And say : that our sole ground for believing God to be true,
Is, because God himself has told us so in a Book.
As though, if we hitherto were doubtful of his truth,
We could safely take his word in proof of his truth.
This is mere puerility, though inveterate in some schools,
And paraded by men who would be eminently logical.
   But the Truthfulness of God is not shown in letters and words,
But pervades all nature and the mind of man.
His Rectitude undoubtedly forbids him to deceive us;

Therefore never can he have given us lying and delusive Faculties.
No minds at all could he give us, save minds adapted for truth;
Not indeed seeing everything, nor omniscient of the smallest thing,
Nor incapable of error, nor independent of culture.
Fallacies stand around us, as dangers in all life,
To be avoided and guarded against by rightful industry.
But our minds and instinctive judgments cannot be essentially delusive,
If the God who gave them is truthful and loves our truthfulness.
Thus that, which was made a *Presumption* on the threshold of Science,
Recurs, reaffirmed, as a noble principle in religion,
Displaying harmony unsought, but such as is common in Truth.

BLESSEDNESS OF GOD.

Every true Theist, seeing all our powers in God,
Force, Intellect, Desire, and Judgment and Will,
Inevitably judges that in him they are all perfect,
Absolute in completeness and also absolute in harmony:
Hence *Peace* and *Blessedness* are ascribed universally to God,
Not by Induction, nor by Experience, which here apply not,
But by Intuition, and by Deduction from prior truths.
Even Epicurean fancy painted its gods as Blessed,
Enjoying serene peace retired in time eternal:
But Epicurus vainly thought that the peaceful must be inactive,
And, lest anxiety impair bliss, removed mortal cares from God.
No such puerility under modern science is possible.
To the strong of body or mind activity brings pleasure;
To the wise and self-knowing, government is unanxious;
On the infinite in power infinite burdens sit light.
And as every faculty, rightly exerted, brings its own delight,
And the nobler the faculty, the purer its breath of joy;
And as man knows man by sympathy only, by presumptive likenesses,
Attributing inward sameness where outward sameness appears;
So, concerning the Unseen and Eternal heart, we judge fitly
That it rejoices as we rejoice, only with joy far more glorious,
In exerting energies like to ours, but more glorious than ours by far,
Grander, mightier, completer, harmonious, eternal.
Therefore has man's universal voice pronounced God BLESSED:
And to believe his perfections is to ratify the verdict.

THE LOVE OF GOD.

There is a certain kindness which a man has for brutes:
Life and happiness he would wish for all innocent creatures,
Though he scruple not to take life for small convenience.
For the death of his horse or his dog he might sincerely grieve,
Yet not long nor fondly, as with sacred remembrance.
But where love has been mutual between moral beings,—
Intelligent love, founded on virtuous esteem,—
More sacred is the sentiment, and far more lasting.

Now all who believe in God the Righteous at all,
Are sure of his *kindly* feeling to all mankind:
Yet how intimate is that feeling, all are not agreed.
For some will say, that "as a man loves his beast,
With a certain vague kindliness, so does God love man:
The disparity of nature forbids a closer friendship:
They stand off at arm's length, and embrace not intimately.
God desires a noble creation, as a duke a troop of deer,
Careless of the individuals, careful only of the herd,
Which is perpetuated in beauty, though each is short of life."—
Such a theory is self-consistent, intelligible, worthy of debate;
It is the view of philosophic intellects, but hardly of the most pious.

Nor is this wonderful; if, as perhaps it may here be shown,
The doctrine deals fatal blows to spiritual piety:
And we trust also to show that it is not well-grounded.

Recalling first principles, we find that God in Conscience
Enjoins certain duties and endless progress in virtue,
With such feelings toward himself as his nature demands.
If now, through the disparity of his nature and ours,
He stand far apart and embrace us not intimately,
Yielding to us no love, he surely demands no love.
As well might a man claim love from his cows or sheep.

Love is our highest and most holy virtue:
If God has it not as much as we, how can he be all lovely?
Love is of all our affections the most glorious,
Supplying forces and heart to every noblest virtue.
To deny then that the Source of love has love is mere paradox,
And has no claim to pass as cautious philosophy,
But tends to degrade God as less virtuous than man,
Making adoration of his Holiness impossible,
And depriving the soul of the right or drawings to love him.

Thus spiritual worship and all heavenward motives fail,
Unless God's love to man be definite and personal;
Enthusiasm becomes gratuitous and self-devotion an imprudence,
And religion loses its motives and its highest energies.

Nor only so, but Prayer becomes hardly reasonable.
For if the Highest regards men generically only,
Designing mankind to thrive, but caring for no one man,
Why should he attend to the personal case of each,
Or answer his prayer, or assist his struggling virtue?
And if he stand apart from us, as a man from his cattle,
Spending no love on each and requiring no love,
No communion of soul between God and man is appropriate:
Rather would the attempt be unseemly and presumptuous.

This is perhaps the secret belief of many acute persons,
(For it flows direct from the denial of God's love,)
And they accept our conclusion, as right and natural.
Thus their religion wholly loses its inward element;
And even if they imagine some future existence for man,
God will in it be eternally separate from man still.
Such a scheme may be styled religious; nevertheless internally
It has no more spiritual force than has moral Atheism.

Like Atheism also it is opposed to primary facts.
God does not stand at arm's length and deal with us *from without*,
As a king with subjects, and keep no personal converse:
But he speaks to us *within*, he whispers in our hearts.
As a Soul within the soul is he closely interfused,
Not dealing as by edicts issued to a multitude,
But by private counsel as from a friend to a friend.
And all those principles, which we laid down as Axioms,
Show that God commands individual virtue,
And approves personal adoration, personal communion.
And since the human heart is notoriously capable of this,
Our proper relation to God is not as that of brutes to man.
Nor does he value us for our Usefulness as a man values sheep,
While we in turn look to him for Protection only;—
(As in the relations of the unlike, where unlike benefits are sought,
And Virtue is not sought, or is but a means to an end;)—
But here Virtue itself begins and ends the relation;
Hence the affection arising is that of proper friendship.
We love him for his Goodness, *he* loves us that we may be Good:
Thus we are humble friends of him the Supreme Friend,

And self-devoting adoration of his Holiness becomes possible.
  Atheism which denies Intellect, must deny Virtue to God;
But every form of Theism, which holds God to be righteous,
Must teach that our goodness is but a shadow of his goodness,
And that our deepest love to him but hints his love to us.
In this very way does the heart which loves him learn his love,
And his true worshipper rises above philosophic doubts.
  Finally, Love is to us the deepest fountain of Joy,
Which surpasses by far the delights of Knowledge and Honour:
And though we claim not entire acquaintance with the Highest,
Nor may say that he lacks bliss, if one source of bliss be dry,
Yet if we may trust in the analogies of Earth and Heaven,
Our noblest joy can hardly be joy unknown to God;
And he, who is blessed beyond all creature-blessedness,
Must abound in that personal Love, whence flows our most blessed bliss.

SIN AND HOLINESS.

  Honest sceptics have said: "Talk not of Sin and of Holiness:
Right and Wrong I understand,—the expedient and the reasonable,—
But the Holy and the Sinful are as cloudy as the Soul and as God.
I love not to be mystical: fly heavenward, if you can;
I, whether from wisdom or weakness, cling to the solid earth."
  Let us welcome candour and plain confessions,
As better for truth than self-ignorance and pretension;
Nor would any wise physician scold down the patient,
Who honestly tells his symptoms, whether of health or of disease.
  Yet dry were the morality, which taught nothing of reverence,
Nothing of tender sentiment or of sacred consciousness.
Let us for a moment contemplate, how needful are these ideas,
Which the hearts of all nations have expressed in language.
  If our parents have well earned love and honour,
Watching over our childhood and training us to manhood,
Seems it not fit to *revere* their loving kindness?
When death has torn them away, is it a mawkish folly
To dwell tenderly on the retrospect and count it *sacred?*
Truly this inheres in the noblest hearts,
In hardy and rugged natures, guiltless of mawkishness.

Tender memory of the dead is not cherished because *expedient*,
Nor deign we to justify it, nor do we enforce it as *reasonable*;
Yet *sacred* it remains, shrouded from stranger's sight.
Surely if any avow that he understands Right and Wrong,
But that Sacredness is a word unintelligible and useless,
He has the conscience and sentiment of an unripe schoolboy,
Ignorant of manly morals and of all deep love.

  If ever our heart has been awed into veneration
Of another soul wiser, nobler, and loftier than ours,
If Reverence kindle into Love, truly that love is *sacred*.
Or when brother or husband cherishes sister or wife,
Does he know nothing but right and wrong, nothing of *sacred* feeling,
Like to the dry-souled lad, whose playground is his world?
  Or is a husband satisfied that his wife act lawfully,
With amiable behaviour, outwardly correct,
Without delicate sentiment and purity of feeling?
Will he hold *Pure* and *Impure* to be words unmeaning?
Foolish young men, who are atheists, have made this avowal,
But the heart of mankind unaffectedly condemns it.
  See now how this bears upon Sin and Holiness.
He who from heart seeks virtue, is grieved to fail in virtue,
And sees virtue above him, loftier and purer,
Sacred to him, *revered* by him, as befits the loftier:
And to fall from virtue pains him and humbles him and disgusts him,
As when some odious garbage has defiled the glory of beauty:
Thus fault is to him *impure*, offensive to inward feeling,
And to commit fault wilfully is esteemed Sin and defilement.
And as no heart of woman is lovely to her lover,
Save when of itself it rejects the impure with hatred;
So no soul of man is lovely with the nobleness of manly virtue,
Till it has learned abhorrence of trespass as defiling.
Then is its goodness Holy and its evil is beheld as Unholy.
Not often can such a heart be Atheist: Holiness and God (we admit to you)
Closely are at one in sentiment, not far are parted in belief.
To believe in God is to revere him, and to know that he is all-holy;
To revere him is to rejoice in Holiness and to feel that all wrong is Sin.

THE LETTER AND THE SPIRIT.

"All are not Israel, who are of Israel,"
Proclaimed of old the great apostle of the Gentiles:
Nor is it easy to overlook, that under every creed
Some men are votaries of Goodness, and others votaries of Self:
And though Truth is valuable, and a sounder creed better than a baser,
Yet under a worse creed are sometimes found better men,—
Better than those who join speculative truth with self-seeking.

Many Jews and many Christians have been upright, noble, and holy,
But neither Jew nor Christian asserts that the majority of his brethren are such:
It is confessed that the many have a form without the substance.
The like differences must exist in the heart of religions less known to us.
The like must exist among those who dissent from each religion,
Some through intellectual disgust, others with higher sentiment.
To love goodness and to hate evil everywhere,—
Chiefly the evil in one's self,—is to be really good:
And he who loves goodness, loves God, who is essential goodness,
Even if he discern not God and gravely doubt his existence.
But God exists, despite of man's doubt; and reigns in man's heart,
Whenever any man is subject to the high command of Conscience,
Which is truly God within, though the Atheist know it not:
And to love goodness, and to obey all the law which we discern,
Is better than to believe more fully and to disobey,
Loving self and following sin, in spite of religious notions.
So neither is the Pagan, or a Pantheist whose God is not moral,
Brought nearer to true goodness by his religious creed,
Or nearer to the worship of him in whom goodness is impersonate.
Nay, if they worship an immoral image, discerning its immorality,
Their idolatry is stark rebellion against the true God,
Though it counterfeit religion and use sacred words,
Which the Atheist rejects, perhaps through virtuous honesty.

Among Atheists and Pantheists, and among Theists of every grade,
Good men may be found, and bad men, as in every nation:
Yet as each nation has its character, and one is higher than another,
Higher as to the average, though not always as to individuals,
Not unlike is the comparison between creed and creed.
No class of men is cast away by him whose Spirit pervades us.
Our part it is, to love and choose Truth alway,
But likewise, to love and honour goodness alway,
Under whatever disguise we find it, under whatever ignorance:
For he who loves God for his goodness, cannot but love goodness in man.

EVIL.

Good becomes Evil, in comparison with the Better;
For to do our Best is always the command of Duty.
And Evil becomes Good, when every alternative,
Possible to us *then* and *there*, is only Worse.
Thus Good and Evil are truly relative terms;
And unless all things and all ways were Good alike,
Of necessity some things and some ways are Evil.
Nay, if nothing could be Evil, nothing would be Good,
But all things whatsoever would be indifferent and unmoral.
The possibility of Vice is the condition of Virtue.
So likewise is Evil the revelation of Good,
And Human weakness of Divine strength.
*If we had no lower impulses, no meaner passions,
No drawings toward the worse, no susceptibility of temptation,
Never should we distinguish God's voice in Conscience,
Nor know that God is moral, nor frame moral judgments.
But as the eye which should see all things of a single hue,
Would be wholly inobservant and unaware of that hue;
(For, if everything were green, we should have no word for green,
Not knowing that things were green, nor imagining other possibility;)
But when hues are different, as blue and green and red,
Then the contrast calls attention, and excites comparison,
And creates names, and makes knowledge possible:
So the varieties of action, better and worse possibilities,
Reveal to us Good and Evil, initiate Morality,
And open a window of the soul to acquaint ourselves with God.
Very notable is the error of many professed Theologians,
Who treat of Evil as an unrevealed mystery,
The "entrance" of which into God's world is so marvellous.
But it is not the *origin* nor the *entrance* of Evil,
Which deserves to excite amazement, much less to grieve;
For, its entrance, the experience of it, is essential to moral progress.
But its force, its persistence, its prevalence, its inveteracy,
After the Better has been shown, and is partially acknowledged,
These are what amaze, what afflict, what appal,
And might draw tears of blood, if our hearts could weep rightly.

---

* "Instead of an evil nature, this lower nature of ours is a necessary Postulate of all our Virtue."
—*Essay on Intuitive Morals*, vol. i. p. 96.

Hence also many persons of conscience sensitive and delicate,
Dismayed and shuddering at the evil which they find within,
Have imagined a personal Demon, a spiritual Tempter,
Acting within the Conscience in opposition to God,
As though man's evil were too bad to be his own.
But never can such a thought commend itself to Science.
For if the evil within us is too bad for man,
Much more is it too bad for a mighty superhuman spirit.
If Satan tempts us, who is it that tempts Satan?
Can evil be native to him, and can it not be native to us?
If angels be God's creatures, they are as good as we:
Nor can any devils be plausible, except as uncreated.
If in the great Universe marks be found of two Gods,
A good God and an evil God, alike independent,
Struggling through eternity, alike unconquered;
Then, and then only, may the evil within our hearts
Be plausibly ascribed to the temptations of the evil God.

CHILDISH AND MANLY VIRTUE.

Many a Virtue springs up as a wild flower in the heart of the wild man,
In the heart of the spoiled child, and in the midst of error or crime.
As is the nature of the individual, such is the wild virtue,
A growth of untrained impulse, an untutored fruit,
Natural to the soil, easy to the tree, favoured by the climate.
Thus one man is generous, another is brave, a third is grateful;
One is just, one is tender-hearted and forgiving:
Yet of all these perhaps there is not one but is deliberately vicious;
Not one, who can on the whole be called virtuous, righteous, good.
Such is mere natural virtue, unequable, impulsive,
A fair and kindly product, to be welcomed and rejoiced in.
Happy is the nature that abounds in wild virtue,
Happy the parent and the teacher who have to train such natures.
But this is not yet the true virtue of man: it is a child's virtue at best:
It is as the virtue of a faithful dog, of a brave obedient horse:
It is not self-reflective, self-guiding, deliberately chosen;
It is fragmentary, superficial, unsupported from the depths of the soul,
Nor is it any sure pledge of higher and broader growth.
The manly and genuine virtue is followed with resolve,

Not merely because easy and congenial to the person,
But because he discerns it to be good, and because he will follow the good;
Therefore, whether easy or hard, he chooses the right and noble.
Only thus can goodness overspread the character,
Only thus can virtue aid virtue, and wild virtue be perfected.
For when it grows beside vice, though by its own hardihood it thrive,
Yet is it blighted by evil shade, and tainted by evil odour.
Nay, the generous becomes selfish and cruel, to gratify profligacy;
The brave man trembles as a dastard, lest his embezzlements come to light;
The truthful man becomes false, to save his comrade from punishment.
Thus Vice fights against Virtue, and stifles or cripples it,
And weakens the moral Will, and forbids the virtue to be resolute.
 · Often also a virtue cannot rise loftier, though no vice smother it,
Yet because other virtues are not stout enough to prop it.
Generosity fails, for want of Patience, or of Forgiveness, or of Self-denial;
And Forgiveness fails, for want of Self-knowledge;
And Justice fails, for want of Bravery or of Generosity.
All true virtues spring out of one root, the love of Goodness:
Feed thou and water the root well, and all will flourish together.
And the higher doth *one* rear its branches, the deeper will the fibres strike,
And the stronger will the clump of root grow, and nourish *all* the stems:
Thus the virtues which were fair in their wildness will be robust when fostered.

Moreover when *all* virtue is pursued,—and is pursued *because* it is virtue,—
Then Conscience assumes supremacy, and unveils her righteous power,
And the heart honours the idea of the all-righteous, the all-holy,
And the vision becomes all-lovely and is impersonate as God the Good,
Until the soul worships with love and joy, and finds her Inspirer.
Then at length Virtue reaches her true stature and is no longer childish.

THE MORAL AND THE SPIRITUAL.

Words are not always used with unvarying meaning.
Moral sometimes includes *Spiritual*, sometimes excludes it;
Nor will popular language always endure scientific rule.

But there are men whom we call Moral, and not yet Spiritual;
Who do indeed honour virtue and virtuous men,
And so shun all conscious degradation of the heart,
That for " sacred honour " they will lay down fortune and life;
Yet themselves are aware that Spiritual they are not.

THE MORAL AND THE SPIRITUAL.

What is that which they are not, and wherefore not?
   Their virtue is stationary, little aggressive; resting in its own camp,
Satisfied to beat off the enemy and make no new conquests.
They will not encounter self-reproach; therefore they shun the immoral,
And do good, and are industrious, and honourable, and brave;
But, immersed in useful and praiseworthy pursuits,
Think not to make virtue itself the chief object of pursuit,
Nor study to press forward to virtue always more complete.
They approve virtue, but do not long for it.
   But to him who is Spiritual, the desire of virtue is a *passion*,
Not of this virtue or that only, but of virtue all round,
Whether applauded or not by man, whether seen or not:
And his chase is perpetual, for the quarry cannot be caught,
For the law of his life moves forward, as though he chased his shadow.
Thus to the mere Moral man virtue is Finite,
And to the Spiritual man virtue is an Infinitude;
And the Moral man often rests in the aims of earth and time,
But the Spiritual tends ever toward the Infinite God.
   For the passion, which gnaws his bosom at his own failures,
Shows him, as a God within, the rebuker of his wanderings,
And reminds him of that eye divine which judges righteously.
And contrariwise, he who ponders for what God has made us,
Beginning from the moral, learns to be spiritual,
If sincerely he try to please God, to live under his eye,
To shun every evil weakness and to count offence a Sin.
And hardly may any one be spiritual, except thro' religion's force,
By intercourse with the most Holy, and consciousness of his presence.
   An Atheist has written, that such language *is cloudy and mystical*:
But nowise admit we that it may fitly be called cloudy;
Mystical perhaps it is, as is all hidden love and sorrow.
   The Astronomer is ever aware of the presence of Gravitation,
And the Electrician sees all things pervaded by Electricity;
Powers descried by the mind, unwitnessed by any sense,
Long unknown to the wise, still undiscerned by the vulgar:
Yet this perception of things hidden is not esteemed cloudy.
   Not less distinctly descry we an Omnipresent Mind,
Not less clearly apprehend that that Mind beholds us,
And searches our hearts and is conscious of our motives,
And disapproves our evil, and approves our good.
Hourly to feel his presence, his observance, his judgment,
Comes only by meditation and exercise, and by shunning distraction;

Yet is it highly rightful, reasonable, intelligible, not cloudy.
  Unclouded and serene will the sight of God's countenance be,
When we hunger after virtue with all our heart and soul,
And, with mind unsuperstitious, *know* that a Holy Lord
Approves our poor efforts and looks on them with complacency:
Then consciousness becomes dialogue, teaching us his replies.
  Would the Moral learn to be Spiritual, or the Spiritual to be blessed,
Let him change the chase after Virtue into the study to please God.
Let him cherish constant Reverence, till Reverence blossom into Love.
Sweet is the approval of a parent, sweet his silent eye;
But to him who feels how lovely is the Holy Perfect One,
What is sweet as his approval, when the open heart knows of it?
Then the spiritual is he who loves God the Spirit,
Ever present, all knowing, a Judge severe and tender.

INSTRUCTION IN VIRTUE.

  Virtue has three kinds of instruction, from Precept, Experience, and Example.
  Precepts are delivered by the Preacher, by the Moralist, by the writer of Books.
No man overlooks that which is obvious, the instruction of direct teaching:
And some who least listen to the Teacher, suppose him the only Instructor,
And believe the precepts of virtue to be a law from without,
Stamped on the brain by authority foreign and untested,
Nor are aware that all the sanction is from the verdict of man's conscience.
Thus they magnify the Church and the Creed and the Priest and the Book,
And look no deeper than the surface, yet learn many wholesome truths.
  But Instruction is also earned by each man in his own *Experience*,
In the wear and tear of life, in sorrow and in joy,
In the wrestlings of temptation, by the warnings of prudence,
From the perplexities of error and from the strength of inward freedom,
By the visitings of God's good spirit, by the earnestnesses of prayer,
By the love of dear kinsfolk and by the neglect of the heartless.
Each man's experience may be narrow, yet no instruction pierces so deep;
None gives conviction so unshakable or strength so abiding.
  But if Experience be narrow, it is widened by *Example*,
It is roused, it is kindled, it is blown into a flame.
The child learns less from the parent's precepts than from the parent's life,
From the deeds done carelessly, from the words dropt casually,
From the unstudied outbursting of inward character.

The man who is apathetic to goodness, hardened in worldly incredulity,
Supposing virtue to be a fable and religion hypocrisy,
Admires the simple goodness of the virtuous and unconscious poor.
Nay, he respects the philanthropist who sacrifices wealth and ease,
Though he continue blind to all goodness which enjoys outward good.
The Example of virtue is the best Instructor.
A Religion whose example pleads not its cause, is decaying and about to die.
　But not of virtuous men only are the examples useful,
Nor is the example of the vicious chiefly useful in his vice,
Or the example of the thoughtless in his thoughtlessness and error.
To the student of virtue Wild Virtues are an example,
The sweet wild flowers that bloom in common homes,
In the cottage of the peasant, in the boat of the fisherman,
In the rash heart of the sailor, the pagan or the savage.
Beneath the trader's hard outside, or the lawyer's subtle falsehood,
Amid the recklessness of gaiety, under the purple of royalty,
Much may the wise man learn from the example of the foolish.
Often may the virtuous take shame at the virtues of the vicious,
And the teacher go to school at the foot of the pupil.
Virtue and Science are unscrupulous whence they draw their wholesome lessons,
From the dark chambers of iniquity, from the loathsome abodes of filth.
For, their selective touch transmutes and purifies,
And all things to them become pure, and all things holy;
So they suck sweetness out of the spoiler, and "despoil the Egyptians."

OBJECTS OF TEACHING.

　Animals, as they are more intelligent, may more receive man's training,
Who teaches them to fear his displeasure, to honour his superiority,
To understand his indications and perform his commands.
Thus are the horse and the ass and the camel commonly trained,
Thus in some measure the ox, but still more the elephant.
But these for the most part are made only intelligent tools,
Which exert no judgment, but merely do as they are bid.
　Higher is the culture, where judgment is exercised;
As when the sagacious mule learns to pick his own paths,
And laden unnaturally, on an unnatural country,
By memory and observation and judgment attains safety.
Or as when the shepherd's dog, uncommanded by his master,

Runs to save a sheep from danger which he foresees.
Only few of the lower creatures can thus be trained:
It belongs to nobler powers, and it is pre-eminent in Man.
    Man possessing Free Will, is made for Judgment:
Made for the exercise of judgment, and made to be judged.
To train man as a mere tool, may belong to special industries,
A temporary necessity not to be reproved.
Hand-skill is often but habitual and mechanical,
Nor other is the aptness which the soldier gains by drill:
But if life had no other training, life were not worth much.
    Moreover it is visible, that as higher Invention grows,
We use powers without us to perform mechanical acts,
And hereby relieve fellow-men from tedious drudgery.
Tame cattle first began the long career of civilization,
Which fire, wind, water and steam are continuing.
And even where these are not available, yet the wise know well,
That one who works with *judgment* is far better than a tool;
As the soldier who has patriotism, zeal, forethought, calculation,
Is worth more than a well-drilled obedient wooden machine;
And in a healthy society Judgment is better paid than Routine,
As more fruitful in high results, and more eminently human.
Knowledge is not always a training of man's mind,
For one may know much, and remain very foolish and very weak;
But knowledge of each subject is needful to sound judgment.
Nevertheless, even so, the Faculty is more valuable than the Knowledge;
For the knowledge is the means and the faculty is the end;
And the chief end of sound training is to impart *new Power*.
Nor does the teacher train the pupil merely to submit to orders,
To believe on authority and to receive knowledge;
But to exert his faculties, and to attain skill in using them.
Even where Judgment has the narrowest field, the same thing appears;
For even the mathematician trains his pupils to be his equals,
Yea, if possible, to be his superiors: to win all his results
More easily than he himself won them, and to start with advantage,
Earlier armed with high power, and wider of survey.
    So neither would the wise painter impart a mere routine of skill,
Or limit the love of beauty to his own few tastes and powers:
But would teach the pupil to cherish delicate perception;
Then, as sight and feeling and love all grow, so will he execute better,
And love will teach discrimination, and hand-work will feed love.
Thus even in pursuits not Moral, human training spreads wide

Beyond blind receptivity into Power and choice and love.
  But in things properly Moral, the same is pre-eminently necessary
To all manly culture, and even to advancing childhood,
Because of Free Will, which must be trained to choose aright
By the force of sound wisdom, of right loves and right habits.
The Moral and Spiritual teacher has done little, or next to nothing,
Until his words have become *a Power within* the learner;
Until the learner has attained Judgment of his own,
Approving that which is *Right*, and *choosing* that which he approves.
While he is merely receptive and obedient, he is as a child, and without stability.
Hence the noblest aim of spiritual teaching has been " *to minister the Spirit*,"
To impart spiritual powers that may equal or surpass the teacher
Both in knowledge and discernment and also in strength of goodness:
And the teacher who aims not at this, knows not his proper duty.

SELF-CONVICTED TEACHERS.

  The true teacher of religion desires that God may be honoured,
And that man by honouring God may be strengthened and ennobled;
But himself desires no honour, nor that men bow down to him:
Nay, if any bow too humbly, he will be inwardly aggrieved,
Lest the man lose his manhood, and become childish or idolatrous,
Not seeking after God and meeting him in his Conscience,
But making the teacher his mediator and substitute,
A proxy in religion, to screen him from contact with the Holiest.
And every wise teacher, who has experience of mankind,
Knows that idolatry and childishness are deadly bane,
Deadly to religion beyond all other errors,
And to be shunned as pestilence and hideous curse.
Hence the true-hearted teacher, wise in the past,
Will hate with tenfold hatred all self-exaltation;
And would rend his clothes with horror, like Barnabas and Paul,
If honours due to God were tendered to *him:*
And if any fall before him, as Cornelius before Peter,
He will indignantly reprove it, and command them to rise.
Nor will only the outward posture of worship grieve him,
But equally too abject a resting of the heart upon him;
For his task is, to guide men's hearts to God,
Not to intercept God's radiancy and intercept their devotion,

By a double theft cheating both Earth and Heaven.
And if he be truly upright and moderately perfect,
So that a soul be saved to God, he cares not through whom,
Nor will dare to say, that he is himself God's sole channel;
Nor wishes his own name to be heard among men,
God and God's prophet echoing side by side.
Yea, to hear his own self thus coupled with the Eternal,
Should grieve him deep in heart, as a real profanity.

   Little mischief could ensue from impieties even monstrous,
If impiety and monstrosity came forth pure and simple;
For, men's right feeling would reject them, ere they could take root.
But the good mingled with error gives passport to the error,
And is counted as Evidence, and seems to be infallible.
Soon, the votaries forget that the strength of the evidence was finite,
And heap on to the old basis,—as though its strength were infinite,—
New loads, which would have crushed all belief at first.
Thereupon, some men reject the good for the sake of the folly,
And others hold the folly for the sake of the good,
And still more hold the folly and neglect the good,
Which yet aids constantly to defend the folly.
So truly was it said by one of our own wise men,
That Confusion is to truth more fatal than is pure Falsehood.

   Would you judge what religious pretensions are indefensible,
Imagine them now to be propounded new and for the first time.
For as Sin to the habituated loses half her ugliness,
So does False Religion lose half her monstrosity,
Which only a fresh eye can duly estimate.
Thus mankind has alway given easy faith to antiquity,
And every nation sustains its own vain fables,
Believing in manhood the dreams of childhood.
But if *now* a teacher apparently good and holy
Should thrust *Himself* in as an object of religion,
(As a majority in Europe believes, in spite of denial by subtler minds,)
His holiness would be judged but a veil of impiety,
Nor would any defence earn for him a hearing with the wise:
So intense is the conviction that such pretensions are unprovable.
Therefore the self-obtruding teacher is essentially self-refuted.

INDIVIDUALISM AND UNITY.

Where like elements are alike blended, results are alike;
So judge we of ourselves, and so find we many ways confirmed.
Where climate and soil are unchanged, even over broad tracts,
If the seeds of one plant be diffused, the same forms grow up:
And whatever in nature is ruder and more elementary
Remains in all the individuals more constantly like to itself.
But culture, which adds new elements or alters proportions,
Soon brings in changes of aspect, which mark changes within;
Hereby man, in his little day, imitates God's great action.

Thus the herbs which in hedges or on the wild moor
Disclose flowers small and tender-hued, each like to each,—
The same, if planted in gardens, with rich mould often stirred,
Under moisture and warmth grow quickly stronger and brighter,
And put forth flowers larger, many-hued, flaunting in richness.
Nor do the garden plants differ from their wild brethren only,
But also among themselves great variety is seen,
Unless the gardener, with fixed purpose and industrious art,
So admeasure every new element as to gain uniformity.

Thus the dogs, which when wild, whether in the streets of a great city,
Or on the free hill-side, are all alike, and no other than the wolf;
The same, if taken into the friendship and families of man,
Win new affections and new habits, with food less uniform;
And as their feelings multiply, so also do the sounds of their voices.
Out of the monotonous whine and howl rises expressive variety;
And among them new tastes spring up, new strivings, new instincts,
As this or that part of their nature happens to be stimulated;
And their very shapes are altered, and their colours, and sizes,
And hair, and voice, though they alway remain dogs.
Such *Individualism* rises out of moral and mental causes,
Joined with much change of habits and some change also of food.
Nor can it be thought that all the result is from mixture of race,
Through the taming of wild dogs from diverse regions.
For, the varieties of wild dog put together from all the world
Will not at all suggest to the eye the special aspects of the tame,
Much less will they display the capacities and voices of the tame.

So also rude tribes of men, who live a savage life,
Differ little one from the other in aspect or in tastes,
Though in force of character and of talents a few may be eminent.
But when culture of the mind begins, diverse tastes are seen,

And great diversity of power and diverse character:
And the features of the face soon mark these diversities,
Nor is savage monotony any longer found in the aspect.
Thus, side by side with improvement, Individualism arises,
And especially in such improvement as is mental and moral.

  For, that part of man which is animal, or indeed vegetative,
Changes little or not at all while culture advances.
Neither length of life nor animal powers nor instincts change,
Save that the civilized differ more in strength than savages.
But as the mind is more complex than the noblest body,
Its elements more numerous and their perfection harder,
So its culture must promote different faculties in different men,
And while each is one-sided, Society is consummate,
Since the lack of each is supplied by the excellence of others.
For, that which is of the mind loses not by being shared,
But multiplies itself when imparted, and cannot be lessened:
Hence the Individualism which advancing culture brings into Each,
Is by a divine ordinance a means of elevating All;
And he who would enforce Uniformity and repress Individualism,
Represses genius, represses taste, represses general morals.

  Morality has its laws, of which many must be sternly enforced,
That Duty may be observed between man and man by all.
But the inner actions of the spirit, which unite man to God,
As they cannot be enforced, and may not be controlled from without,
So do they eminently depend on complex causes and culture;
And each man's moral history differs, as do men's powers of thought:
Great therefore is religious diversity, where religion is real.
If each will help each lovingly, respecting Individualism,
All will be an aid to all, and all will move toward God;
And when Religion shall become Science, disagreements will lessen:
Individualism, as in Science and Art, will remain, without impairing Unity.

LAW AND MERCY.

  Sometimes it is taught that God is a stern avenger of sin,
At other times that he is merciful and rejoices in forgiveness.
Both statements are true, if rightly interpreted;
Nor are they well understood, while they seem at variance.

  God's moral laws are unchangeable, as his laws in nature,

Never violated, though often counteracted by wisdom.
Every sin and every error has its natural results,
Its peculiar penalty, to be borne, but not to be evaded.
According as every man soweth, so likewise doth he reap;
Nor can we get wheat from thistles, or apples from gorse.
Indulge in negligence, and you will not reap the rewards of industry:
Sow the seeds of malice, and you must look for a crop of hatred;
But the loving heart that sows tenderness, reaps affection.—
As water drowns and fire burns, so every passion does it own work,
Nor does God relent at man's cry, and suspend his wise laws.
Crime and sin are not always punished just as we expect,
And hearts and houses are often shrouded from our sight:
But seeing what we do see of the tendency of sin,
And the countless calamities entailed by mere error,
We cannot but account God to be inflexible in severity,
Stern to condemn sin and to recall us from mistake.

Nevertheless, as poisons have their antidote,
And as diseased flesh may be burnt out and a limb be made healthy;
So is the disease of sin burnt out of the soul by repentance,
Though the outward results of the sin may remain to plague us.
And as an old sore in the body, while it remains sluggish, will not heal;
But if it be wakened into pain, so that it throbs with hot life,
Then, if the body can bear the fiery heat and agony,
The evil is often worked off, and the wound is healed:
So does Repentance inflame and heal the old sores of the Soul:
Nor is any sin so pleasant, but repentance is vastly more painful,
A divine retribution most just and adequate.

Outward stripes are laid on an offender who has no inward sorrow;
Such punishment is a coarse inefficient human substitute.
But when the offender is truly, deeply, certainly penitent,
Then all just hearts know that he has his full punishment,
And desire no further infliction, but forgive his offence,
Receiving him back into kindness:—and this we call *Mercy*.
If Human Law cannot remit the punishment proclaimed,
It is because it cannot discern between hypocrisy and penitence:
But over this we mourn as over inevitable calamity.

And God too is Merciful, though his laws are unchangeable.
The outward effects of sin take their course against us,
Except so far as our repentance may naturally change them.
But when the poison of sin no longer disorders the soul,
He readmits us to his presence, and forgives the past.

Nay, nor does he minutely count up the pangs of repentance,
And strike a balance against the pleasure of sin;
For, many have come back to him by forgetfulness, when sin is worn out.
But none may count upon this; none may hope to forget,
Nor know how bitter remembrance shall hereafter arise.
The deeper our knowledge, the deadlier our wilful sin.
Fear thy own weakness: tremble at the most High: for his very Mercy is severe.

DEATH.

The body of man is visibly like that of the animal,
Made for life and for health, but also for death;
And death was earlier than man, in those countless ages,
When monstrous reptiles pre-occupied the yet-steaming mud:
Nor can it reasonably be thought, that death is a fruit of sin,
When death is ostensibly the condition of all animal life.
Premature death is unwelcome to the strong and happy,
Whom nature urges to cherish life for worthy service:
But when strength is utterly spent through age or disease,
Death is not unwelcome to man, but is a rightful rest,
To the outworn body a relief and not a pain.
Nor has the grave any terrors to nature, be it early or late;
Nay,* "there is no passion so weak, but it conquers death.
"Revenge triumphs over it, Love makes light of it,
"Honour aspires to it, Grief flieth to it,
"Fear pre-occupieth it, tender Pity hath provoked many to it,
"Some, neither valiant nor wretched, desire it from Tedium."
Premature death leaves many dear ones to mourn for us,
And all violent death is girt with terrors,
Which yet are daily borne bravely by brave men and women,
Not signal in virtue, under every clime and creed.
Fear of an after-world comes upon a guilty conscience,
Chiefly when inflamed by the follies of superstition,
Which teaches that God is more merciful now than hereafter,
Or less near to the living than to the disembodied dead,
And suggests to the guilty, that the less he has of God, the better,
And warns him not to rush into God's "nearer presence."
Such teaching would make cowards of the multitude of men,

---

* Bacon's Essay on Death.

Forbidding any but the saintly bravely to expose life;
Nor dares any one to preach it to an embattled army.
Far truer is the instinct of every simple mind,
That no bad soul can endanger itself by right action;
And that when Virtue claims exposure to deadly danger,
Even the guiltiest does wisely in bravely welcoming death.
And as any noble passion, kindled in a guilty soul,
Raises its capacity of virtue, if but for a moment,
And, burning up meaner vice, illumines the man;
So have all times felt, that even the baser in mind
Earn a portion of glorious virtue in dying for their country.
How much rather should the thoughtful, the pious and pure of heart
Happily resign soul and body to the God who gave them,
When necessity or virtue call them to lay down life?
Nor is other faith needed, than the faith of Columbus,
Who, tho' Ocean, fathomless, illimitable, changing into seaweed,
Seemed to part him for ever from his brothers of mankind,
And tho' the magnet itself swerved, knew he still was in God's realm:
For, what if Nature's laws altered? they were yet the laws of God.
So too, if the laws of Being prove new beyond death,
If the soul then find itself bound by new conditions,
Yet it cannot be under any rule other than God's rule,
Nor will God be less tender, less equitable than now.
The darkness of futurity can be no reason for terror,
But much reason for serving actively in our present daylight,
While we know the powers granted us for a scanty time.
Life is good, and Death is good: both are from God;
Excellent in their own hour, pregnant with a hidden future.

ENFORCEMENT OF RULE.

On earth we find, that when High Power is joined with Goodness,
Power exerts itself forthwith for distant Moral purposes,
In which peculiarly human Government consists.
So soon then as men believe that a Supreme Power is intelligent,
Is wise and moral and commands our morality,
(And that he does really command it, Conscience is our witness,)
Forthwith a belief arises in some *Moral Government* of God.
The doctrine was never founded on Historical Experience,

Nor could it ever affect to be a truth of Induction,
Except where knowledge is narrowest and thought puerile:
And hardly can we pretend to know our own selves so well,
As to found on our own history the vast generalization,
Which announces God's Moral Government of the universe,
Firm as may be our belief in the Uniformity of Law.
But mankind has felt it to be an inference inevitable,
That the Power which regulates and upholds the universe,
If he attend to moral action and approve of virtue,
Must regulate and uphold moral affairs likewise;
Although the *mode* of this Government remain debateable.

Where power and deliberate command are joined,
Some *enforcement* of the command was confidently expected:
Else, what earnestness of moral purpose could we ascribe,
If the powerful allow his rightful commands to be scorned,
His wise designs to be marred, his obedient servants to be crushed?
Yet experience shows that God's Government is *not* by "Enforcement,"
And that the idea itself is a delusion drawn from man's feebleness.
Punishment is *not* "Enforcement," though men so name it;
For it comes after the offence, and affects the future only.
Whatever the Omnipotent "enforces," is necessarily fulfilled,
And if he enforced righteousness, sin would be impossible,
Nor would moral freedom remain, but we should be as machines.
Also *if the magistrate could prevent, never would he punish.*
If he looked on inactive, allowing offence under his eyes,
Intending to punish afterward, he would himself be guilty.
Such conduct has no likeness to God's almighty wisdom.

Nor may we compare the All-Wise to a perverse schoolmaster,
Who winks on faults at present, and threatens distant penalty.
Then the children, bent on sport and borne by reckless folly,
Run from frolic into fault, from fault into offence,
And proud of impunity, carry offence into full crime.
Thus the sin, which, while tender, might easily have been stayed,
Becomes hardened and unyielding to mild remedies.
Cruel were the judgment day, bloody the assizes,
Which should call children to trial for a year's unchecked riot!
Never will we justify such a trainer, or choose such a tutor,
Or count his preposterousness a type of heavenly wisdom.
The efficacy of all punishment is in proportion to its nearness,
And it corrects the offender best, when it follows the offence close.
God's punishments must be perfect, and perfectly fitted to us,

Suited to our Free Will, and also to our shortsightedness.—
Since nearness is a good in penalties, especially on the shortsighted,
His penalties must follow upon guilt at once:
And if punishment, delayed till after death, be credible,
Unseen, unknown, dimly understood or believed,
Least of all assuredly does it *enforce* righteousness.
Whatsoever retributions a future life may reserve,
They cannot involve principles condemnatory of the present.
All God's doings are perfect, and this world is of his making,
Nor does it abound with blunders hereafter to be mended.
The future, whatever it be, will be a growth out of that which is,
Not an overthrow and convulsion, nor a confession of past anarchy.

 That God is a Moral Governor, is certain to every Theist,
But that he governs *alway*, is surely no less certain:
Nor can any one without extravagance and self-confutation
Urge present anarchy as a proof of future rule.
Nay; and as he governs alway, so does he judge alway,
Not on one day only, nor with the machinery of a tribunal,
But by eternal law, unseen, self-executing, relentless.

FAITH AND FORESIGHT,

 The shepherd of Chaldæa in days far distant
Foreknew by the stars the coming of summer or of winter:
The savages in Oceanic Islands have sure foreknowlege of the tides,
Both when they will be at highest, and when at lowest;
Guided not by Experience only, but also by Faith.
For, long since have acute sceptics instructively taught and proved,
That Experience of the past avails not for knowing the future,
Unless Uniformity of Natural Law be *presumed*,
Which has no direct demonstration, and is at first matter of Faith.
Yet this *Faith gives foresight* to the untaught and unphilosophic,
And the reasoner, who disowns it, is but foolish or insane.

 Where laws are more complex and experience less uniform,
Though Foresight becomes less exact, yet Faith still gives foresight.
On what day winter-cold will begin, we know not exactly,
Nor can we certainly say, that next winter snow will fall;
Yet we believe in winter rains and provide against winter cold,
Not the less, though ignorant on what day they will set in;

Only madmen can disown the faith which leads to the foresight.

Some moral laws are as uniform as the laws of the atmosphere,
Though in neither case has man's intellect unravelled their tangle,
So as to predict with accuracy and without reservation:
Yet many who think themselves statesmen and politic,
Having no Faith in moral law, behave as foolish or insane,
Because their lack of Faith makes vain their Foresight.

As when an Imperial Power, wishing to make sure its conquests,
Sets at nought Truth and Equity, stirs up Hatred and Revenge,
Cares only to seem strong, and dreads nothing but contempt,
Seeking to crush by violence and inspire awe by might.
The statesmen who advise this, believe in gold and in steel,
Believe in man's cupidity, in his fear and his meanness,
But believe not in God's rule, nor in men's deeper passions.
So in their pride they forget that the strongest have hours of weakness,
Hours, in which those who should succour them, will stab them.
Alway to be strong is impossible: those who do not seek to be esteemed,
Must pay ten times over for all that Justice would have cost,
Or lose that fabric of empire for which they despised God.

He who has Faith in God's laws, knows that Injustice will breed Hatred,
And that, sooner or later, the harvest of Hatred is reaped,
Though he knows not exactly when or how and through whom,
As neither on what day and with what wind the snowstorms will come.
Faith makes the moral man wiser than the immoral statesman,
Enabling him to predict things to which the other is blind.

The vaster our field of survey and the more distant the time,
The less can details be foreseen, and the vaguer is sound prediction:
Yet the principle is the same of all Foresight rising out of Faith.
Of this and of that country we cannot know all the details,
As neither can we know the stores of electricity and of cold:
Hence no certain prediction of pending events is possible:
But the wider the scale of affairs, the surer is moral foresight;
Because, on the wider scale, the broader laws bear sway,
Visible and dominant amid smaller disturbances.
That "a well-governed realm will prosper," we presume:
That "proud and silly power will ruin itself," might be an axiom;
While we pretend not to define how prosperity or ruin shall come.

"God's Kingdom is well governed:" this is most sure,
To those who believe that he has any government at all.
"God's Kingdom must prosper," is the certain augury of Faith;
"The Kingdom of Evil must fall," is a safe prediction:

FAITH AND FORESIGHT.

How soon, we know not: let not our misconduct uphold it!
But by belief in morality the simple are made wise.
To discern broad certainties, which the cunning overlook:
Faithlessness is folly, and discerns not the future.
If nothing else is foreseen by Faith, yet so much is foreseen,
That God who abhors the wrong, means to establish the right,
That Evil must wear itself out, and Good bear final sway,
That the Future is big with blessing, which the triumph of Good shall unfold.

RETRIBUTION.

Retribution plays undoubtedly a large part upon earth,
And guilt punishes itself through the divine ordination.
Some sins more than others entail their own penalty,
Balking the sinner of his prize and of hoped-for enjoyment.
In which result we oftentime feel stern joy,
As, when the spoiler of the innocent is in turn despoiled,
And man's Conscience applauds, and says, "It is deserved."
If this come about by the force of normal causes,
All Theists must ascribe it to a supreme Providence.
  But others go beyond, and lay down an abstract principle,
That Justice demands SUFFERING as a retribution to SIN,
Not to deter or to remedy, but even as *compensatory*.
But herein are wrapt inextricable tangles.
For Suffering and Sin have no common measure,
Nor in abstract thought is "equivalence" imaginable.
And as none could say that a Mile is equal to Ten Ounces,
Or that a Year is equivalent to Fifty-Horse-Power,
(When Space and Weight, Time and Force differ in kind,)
So neither can a Tooth Ache be an equivalent for a Lie,
Nor can any abstract law of Justice decide the *Pains*,
Which shall weigh even in the balance with a certain *Sin*.
Pain and Sin differ in kind, just as Time and Space,
Also we see in God's world a denial of equivalences.
Some faults punish themselves with distressful rigour:
Other guilt, coarser and viler, scarcely earns penalty at all,
Save that of being hardened into a fouler state,
Without pain to the guilty, or conscious degradation:
So various is the amount of Retribution incurred.

Thus the doctrine of abstract relation is proved futile,
Alike by theory and by practical evidence.
   But again, it is assumed, contrary to fact and truth,
That Suffering is, in itself, remedial of Sin.
Contrariwise oftener Suffering is a cause of Sin :
It hardens the heart, and is not normally remedial.
Constraint, not *Suffering*, is the great means of training ;
But as in the treatment of maniacs, so it is with the guilty,
That Constraint, to be effective, must not be too painful.
Let a criminal be so atrocious, as to deserve death and torture,
Yet life with torture will only harden him the more :
Kindness and Constraint combined, alone give hope of remedy.
Never then can JUSTICE claim pains and torture
Growing in intensity proportioned to guilt,
When the punishment can but exasperate the evil,
And, if continued, make sin eternal.
Justice may require the removal, the destruction of the sinner,
For Justice abounds with hatred of guilt and with zeal :
Hatred seeks destruction of that which it hates,
Only *Anger* and *Malignity* demand pain and suffering.
God's government is undoubtedly at war with Sin,
And his battle must prevail, to extirpate and banish it.
Why is not this a Divine Government as glorious,
Without futile vengeance which is fierce too late.

DIVINE GOVERNMENT.

   If Conscience is the voice of God within,
It is a guide to the Government of God without,
And the true interpreter of Conscience discerns divine purposes.
But one in whom Conscience is unripe and confused,
He naturally and necessarily misinterprets the divine reign.
   Most are familiar with the error of expecting present Retribution,
Once fostered even by the wisest, still common with the many.
And because this error seems to be a dictate of Intuition,
Our confidence in Intuition might hurtfully be weakened,
Could we not clearly unveil the course of deception.
   Our inward law of right is to seek first after Virtue,
And secondarily only to follow Happiness :

Whether for ourselves, or for others, we account Virtue the chief good.
But because a chief mode of attaining personal virtue
Is, to guide our conduct rightly towards others;
And because rather by sympathy than by introspection
Comes the early culture of moral thought;
Our duty towards others at first swallows up all virtue.
Now if one man excelled others as a parent excels a child,
One might choose *Virtue* for others rather than Happiness:
For, this is the higher law, wherever practicable.
But seldom can one choose for another, or dream to guide him;
Hence in practice we solely choose *the Happiness* of others,
And the illusion creeps in, that Happiness is the Chief Good.

Out of this illusion rises new error concerning the Divine Rule.
Because each good man chiefly seeks others' Happiness,
(Since to seek for their Virtue is too high an aim,)
Therefore it is thought, that God also must study our Happiness chiefly.
But this is to forget his superior and mighty relation,
And that he, as a parent, can study for our Virtue,
Not being limited, as man is, in action toward fellow-man.
Hence the error that a Divine Ruler will suppress violences,
And by rewards and punishments keep things smooth,
As a human king promoting his subjects' happiness:
And when by painful facts this is signally disproved,
Divine Rule is disbelieved, and all Faith is shaken.
Faith revives, when we discern that Virtue is the chief good,
And is *in fact* promoted by the divine ordinances:
To establish Virtue, is the true end of God's Government;
But by "enforcement" it would be annihilated, not established.

Undoubtedly there remain things obscure and heart-gnawing.
It is not the wreck of Happiness, but of Virtue, which appals.
Injury is bad enough, but depravation by injury is worse;
As when the persecuted becomes revengeful, fraudulent, ferocious,
In which result none can imagine a divine purpose.
Nay, worst of injuries is the corruption of the innocent:
Whether, as when the violent drags others into his crimes,
Or the subtle villain tangles them into guilt and debasement.

Many a time have such things wrung the meditative heart,
Nor does it avail to deny them or to turn away the eyes.
Yet the evil which we hate, God hates far more intensely:
This we cannot but believe, while we believe in God at all.
Therefore we cling to the conviction, that he orders amid disorder,

And that evil is permitted only for the sake of higher good.
Here surely we need Faith; and of Faith we have more to say.

COLLECTIVE GOVERNMENT.

In God's natural forces, mechanical and chemical,
If separately viewed, no moral purpose appears;
For they subserve wickedness as freely as goodness,
And often inflict dire calamity on the innocent.
Take them collectively; view nature as a whole;
And beyond a doubt they must be judged wise and good,
Contributing in harmony to a vast and perfect scheme.
On this then alone many thoughtful minds would rest,
That the Highest has planned only for the absolute whole,
And wisely sacrifices details for the *Average* of good.
Such *alone* they regard to be God's Moral Government.
    On the opposite it is alleged by the general voice,
And by most of the specially religious, that this cannot be *all*;
But that the whole is perfect by the perfection of the details:
And that this alone beseems High Power and Wisdom,
So far at least as all Moral Right is concerned:
That this alone moreover suits physical analogies.
For, the philosophers themselves who admire the Order of the universe,
The Beauty of the earth, the Grandeur of the skies,
The outspread of mighty Life adapted to its circumstances,—
These philsophers teach us that the small is as perfect as the great;
The same forces collect a diamond and a starry cluster,
The same forces are in a raindrop and in the vast ocean.
Nay, that every part is as perfect as the gorgeous whole,
The researches of the microscope do strongly assure us.
If then God govern morally at all, shall we not find his government
Alike on the narrowest theatre and in the mightiest events?
Does not the noble march of Science vehemently recommend us
To have Faith in such analogies, and to abide by them fearlessly?
    Besides, when we ask, *What* is the great and Mighty Whole,—
Spread out immeasurably both in Space and Time,—
It appears, that to provide for it, and for it alone,
Is to postpone indefinitely the welfare of every part.
This is a calamity often endured by great empires,

But does not offer a type of celestial government.
If Ireland complains, the reply is not satisfactory,
That her evils are contingent on the state of parties in England.
Bengal may suffer, because we have just conquered Scinde,
Or Bengal with Scinde, because we have to conquer Burmah;
When possibly any one country might have been well ruled,
If its rulers had not been distracted by foreign cares.
But who will ascribe such infirmity to God,
Or make it our calamity to be subjects of his vast empire?
If in one country injured innocence has no redress,
Shall it be said,—this is winked at by wide-sighted wisdom,
Whose laws are fixed for the benefit of our whole earth?
Well: but might not thus our globe in turn be sacrificed,
For the wider welfare of the planetary dwellers?
Again, might not the good of the solar system give way,
As small in comparison to that of a constellation of worlds?
What then if we sacrifice the benefit of this last
For the whole milky way, or for some grander aggregate?
Even so, we are but on the verge of infinitude,
And infinite *Time* swallows us, just as infinite *Space*.

Since the "Whole" seems, like God himself, to be boundless,
The perfection of the whole lies in perfection of the parts,
And to sacrifice parts to whole were to sacrifice all perfection.
Hence, dark as we may remain concerning God's true Government,
We fall back on the belief that it is a Government of detail,
Aiming at perfection of the parts, and through them of the whole.
Since we know that God in Conscience forbids and warns,
We cannot believe in any neglect under his reign,
Or that individuals are too small for their sins to be noticed,
When they are not too small to receive the commands of his Spirit.
As a spiritual God cares chiefly for individual virtue,
So by training individuals he conducts collective Morality.

FAITH,—TRUST AND BELIEF.

Great mistakes are made on the subject of Faith,
Through doubtful words and traditions of the schools:
And in the hope of aiding to greater clearness of thought,
A full unfolding of Faith, in diverse cases, shall be attempted.

The Faith most familiar to all, is that which we place in a friend,
Whom we trust without precautions, and of whose honour we are sure;
And where facts are doubtful or his conduct unexplained,
We believe without hesitation that the truth will reveal his virtue.

Even in strangers we repose faith, and entrust our lives to them,
As to the captain of a ship, or to a common boatman or driver,
Barely because we know not why they should be cruel,
And because we judge that kindness prevails in untempted man.
Nor is it uncommon to have a trust which suffices for action,
Although it assuredly does not suffice for full belief:
As when, avoiding the dangers of the wilderness,
We trust our lives to a drunken ferryman or wild muleteer;
Or as when we swallow remedies in obedience to a physician,
Though gravely doubting whether his wisdom reaches to our case.
Or as the impetuous hero-king, who drank off the potion,
After handing to the physician the calumnious letter;
And who thereupon watched anxiously the physician's countenance,
To see whether any treason had lurked in his cup.
Here then is a Faith which is *Trust*, but which is not yet *Belief*;
We *trust* upon the probable; but the probable is not yet convincing;
And we do not *believe*, until we are thoroughly convinced.

The necessities of human life enforce upon us such Trust;
For action is often necessary, and time presses,
And wisdom is very limited, and alternatives few;
And we do the thing which seems the least bad of the possible,
Without conviction that it is absolutely to be desired.
Yet Faith is then most perfect when it pervades the whole mind;
When in our action we *trust*, and in our mind *believe*,
So believe, as to suffer no inward struggle or misgiving.

But Faith is not placed solely in persons, nor in moral things;
It has a very wide range over all human action and thought.
Does not the sportsman put faith in the good scent of his hound,
In the strength of his powder, and in his well-known gun,
And the more so, the more he has proved them trustworthy?
Does not the seaman put faith in the seaworthiness of his vessel,
In her obedience to the helm and her power to run close to wind,
To work off from a lee-shore and to lie-to against a hurricane,
Or to scud away before a gale and bear press of canvas?
Does he not entrust life and honour to the instruments of his art,
His compass and log, his sextant, his chronometers,
And his maps which mark currents and shoals and harbours?

Nay, though ignorant himself of the astronomer's high science,
He performs, under bidding, reckonings beyond his understanding,
And trusting to an almanac, infers his longitude,
Believing in the sagacity and truth of his practical rules.
In many of these cases Faith goes *before* experience,
Under guidance of the opinion or faith of others;
But the trust, with belief, grows up into confidence,
When trial and experience confirm its wisdom.
Faith in Nature is easy now; but to a Columbus or a Galileo
To believe in Natural Law might need high courage.

 To *trust* without full *belief* is one-while a folly,
Other-while it marks bravery and noble heroism.
The ship which would run into port through rocks and shallows,
When driven on to some strange shore by an overbearing wind,
Must surely be lost, if the helmsman, through distrust of his map,
Shrink from the nearness of the rocks to which it guides him.
The truth of the map may be uncertain, but his ignorance is certain:
Prudence therefore exhorts to bravery and to strict obedience.
And if, after severe dangers, such obedience has brought safety,
Future faith will be easier, and his bravery be confirmed.
What else is true Bravery than Faith, or Faith than wise Bravery?

 Faith reaches farther still in the history of human thought;
For all philosophy whatsoever begins with Faith,
Faith in the human faculties, Faith that truth is attainable,
Faith in the dominion and uniformity of law.
But at first this Faith is only a *trust* sufficing for action,
And from action rises experience, from experience conviction,
Until sure *belief* is superadded to the primitive trust,
And the faith becomes complete and unhesitating and tranquil.
Faith in the *Uniformity of Law* was at first a guess
Or a presumption or a trust, but has become a firm belief:
And Faith in *Analogy* has inspired the thoughts of genius
And guided them to high discovery and to solid truth:
And Faith in *Simplicity* held astronomers firm,
When faulty observations bade them remodel their doctrines:
Nor is any man fitted for high action or for philosophy,
Who has not a brave faith in principles pervading and immovable,
Which will be eyes to him in the dark, and strength in weakness;—
An instinct mistaken for genius, but more moral than intellectual.

 All Faith in *God's ordinances* is in some sense Faith in God;
But faith in *man's testimony* is in no case Faith in GOD.

This confusion needs to be pointed out and vehemently denounced.
If John tell Peter that he saw some wonderful event, and Peter believe J
This is one man believing another, but has nothing to do with faith in God:
So to call it, is to mislead on a topic vital to religion.
To believe the word of an unknown man on an important matter
Is always dangerous, and never can be meritorious;
Much less can it earn Divine commendation as a fundamental virtue.

   Our trust in men little known soon reaches its limit,
And is shattered by miscarriages or even by one doubtful deed:
But toward one intimately known we justify intrepid trust,
And under events fraught with suspicion we admire it the more.
Therefore the more intimately the heart acquaints itself with God,
The more fully must it trust in God.
Admit then, that the triumphs of sin are direful,
That we do not always see a Providence promoting Virtue:
Is therefore Faith in God's government *baseless* or *unreasonable?*

   Neither baseless nor unreasonable, assuredly is our reply.
The *basis* of our Faith must not be looked for in Induction,—
(This is the fundamental error which ever weakens Faith,)—
But in the inward heart, in pure-minded insight.
Vain is the fallacy, that the wisest human mind
Can grasp the hidden facts of vast moral phenomena,
And judge by the Experience of human history,
What are the moral qualities and secret purposes of the Highest.
Nothing but a rude outline can the ablest thus attain:
Much less is it possible for the millions so to learn of God.
From Conscience alone we learn the Divine Morality;
From Conscience and inward thought, we learn the Divine Government.
On this side we have positive knowledge well-defined,
That the Author of man's heart commands and approves of virtue:
But positive knowledge of God's heart is impossible,
If you seek to ground it on external phenomena.
Nor do Atheists pretend to any well-defined moral results,
But rest in alleging incongruities and uncertainties.
Nothing else could be expected, with our partial minds,
Which see but a fragment of God's vast deeds,—
See but an incomplete outside of moral history.
But we know that unless one suffered by another,
The innocent often by the guilty, mankind would not be one body
With a single life poured through it, nor would affection be called out,
Nor many a noble virtue, which is cheaply bought by suffering.

Much insight into God's purposes has been gained, and more may be gained yet.
If indeed we pretended to make Induction our basis,
And to rest on Historical Experience the belief of Divine Rule,
Then it would be to the purpose to press us with the difficulties,
Which *now* are but difficulties, not refutations.
A burden to Faith they are surely; but strong Faith bears them.
  Nor yet is the belief of God's Government *unreasonable*.
It is the same mysterious Wisdom that orders the outer universe,
As ordains law to the conscience and inspires single hearts:
And when in the stars and planets Wisdom is dominant,
Can the tide of human affairs be borne at random?
And when over winds, waves, wild beasts, mighty Law is supreme,
Does no Law at all control men's crooked will?
Unless behind bad men's deeds a heavenly wisdom rules,
Reason denies that their career could be permitted;—
Disorder in the midst of Order, Lawlessness overriding Law,
Exhibiting God as helpless to train or restrain his creatures.
Or will any one say, that he could not *help* creating them,
But was driven to it by FATE, though foreseeing and hating sin?
Reason and Free Thought,—not Passion and zeal for Creeds,—
Reasonable honour to the Highest and Wisest and Purest,—
Leads straight to the persuasion that a Providence is Supreme,
Supreme over evil men, not to sanction, but to transmute their evil.
It is reasonable that this persuasion mount into a firm conviction:
And we call it FAITH IN GOD, for each and for mankind.
Let it begin with mere Trust, sufficient for faithful action;
It shall end in firm Belief, filling the sore heart with joy.

SPECIAL PROVIDENCE.

  Many talk of Special Providence, and say things not persuasive,
As though the Great Ruler made favourites and dealt arbitrarily,
Or could designedly bless one by the harm of another,
And could pity the hungry lion and overlook the mangled lamb,
Or tamper with his own high laws for small convenience.
Many things have been piously imagined, but unskilfully said,
When we crudely speak aloud strong but dim perceptions,
Powerful already for life-service, but not yet rightly interpreted.

Outward prosperity for the righteous was a hope long cherished,
Suggested by each man's yearning, yet a delusion;
So natural to moral infancy and worldly inexperience,
That poets and writers of fiction, to delight the natural instinct,
Often make Fortune reward goodness, and punish iniquity.

But though Virtue no longer is thought exempt from calamity,
Nor Vice and Injustice certain to meet visible retaliation,
Yet in general it remains deeply fixed in each pious bosom,
That all his life is ordained by Heavenly Wisdom;
The painful events as the pleasant; the lesser as the greater;
So that man may earn virtue out of his daily lot;
And his sorrows or his joys alike be a training to his soul.—
Since each believes this for himself, but is dark as to his neighbour,
Who perhaps neglects virtue;—his own case appears special:
Hence each in turn calls it a *Special* overruling Providence.
The opinion cannot be proved just; but can it be reproved?
It may seem to some a fond fancy, a groundless notion;
Yet it aids to contentment and to pious suggestion,
Filling the heart with sweet thoughts and lofty imaginings;
Nor can it wound charity nor corrupt the laws of rectitude.
If it perhaps be an opinion which no one can *urge* upon another,
Yet, where it is a practical faith, none can *censure* it in another;
And what spiritual instinct persuades with so steady a pressure,
This, if not refuted by fact, it may be unwise to reject.

Nor is it true, that this doctrine puffs up with conceit.
He is conceited already, who thinks that God is for him alone,
And that others, less favoured, are of no concern to the most High.
And, as to the impure man things pure are often impure,
So to the conceited man pious doctrines foster conceit;
As,—that a Providence *so* Special watches over him,
That God has little time or heart to bestow on others.
None confess this to be their thought, yet some appear to think it.
But the reasonable will avow, that no Specialty can exist,
Save so far as the pious are distinguished from the reckless.
When sin increases in the life, and men become worse and worse,
It is hard to say that events are working good unto *them*,
Or that a Special Providence is guiding their feet to *wrong!*
A weakness it may be to separate the Special from the General,
Yet so broad a distinction seems not to feed conceit.

Laying aside needless enigmas, and avoiding pettiness,
Those who know, that Divine Perfection rules all men by One law,

Still trust, that "*in obedience to virtue, come to man what may,
Nothing can hurt him, but all must work together for good.*"
Ascribe this to General or to Special Providence, it is all the same;
Let the wicked act virtuously, and he too may claim his blessing.

   This doctrine, by its own nature, can never wholly be verified,
Verified by the test of fact; for things Future need to be known,
And Good and Evil to be valued, and samples of events discussed
Under difficulties frightful to the Inductive Philosopher.
The doctrine is not believed *in order to* gain support to virtue,
(For then it could give *no* support,) but it is believed for itself,
Because it seems to accord with the merciful equity of God
Not to lay on his creatures commands too hard for our weakness;
And when his claim on our virtue is strict, unexcepting,
We cannot believe that any will lose by obedience;
Or that, when a servant thinks only to fulfil his Lord's command,
That Lord can fail to watch over his servant's interests.
Thus belief in God's equity and goodness suggests the doctrine;
Which roots itself deeper with the deeper growth of morality.

   Besides, we see Peace and Joy to be natural fruits of Holiness;
Natural, yet not uniform; for one suffers *through* another,
And one also *for* another, the strong to uplift the weak.
The virtuous seeks no other reward than Virtue herself,
Yet Holy Happiness is his natural reward;
And to say that it is natural, is to call it God's ordinance.
Does not then Reason suggest a hidden Harmony of things,
Which shall turn into Fact what we see to be Right,
And perfect God's government as absolutely good,
Not merely good in tendency, and good on the whole?

   On such grounds, or on better grounds, the faith stands firm,
That "nothing shall do *real harm* to those who love God."
And a noble aid does it give to our poor struggling virtue,
Calming the fears of prudence without pampering selfishness.

THE MATERIAL AND THE MORAL.

   Pleasant are outward delights to our animal nature.
Not only the more inglorious and soon satiated appetites
Give a natural satisfaction; but much more the insatiable,
Love of motion and activity and every exercise of force,

And the sweet breath of the country, and the sounds and sights of nature.
Such things bring a pleasure and a happiness to lower beings,
And man has his full proportion in the very same pleasures.
We do not undervalue them. When they come in their due order,
We account them pure and excellent and a ground of thanksgiving.
   Useful also are outward appliances to our worldly nature,
The supplies which secure our safety and provide for our comfort,
Which minister to ease or facilitate movement,
Which economize time and multiply the length of life,
Which bring together the absent and widen the mind's survey,
Which confer the gift of leisure, and open the doors of instruction.
Even health and freedom from pain are outward and material,
Equally with disease and wounds, and common to us with the animals.
Only a perverted mind can disparage the precious boon
Of health and strength and leisure and plentiful supplies.
Health and Wealth are glorious advantages, high blessings,
To those who love Virtue better than they love Health and Wealth.
   Yet even the child and the savage know that the deeper pleasures
Only through some *moral* meaning can enter things *material*.
The pleasure of a mother's kiss is earned by the true mother only,
Nor could a stranger's soft lips give to the child the same.
For not from the mere touch and surface does the tender delight come forth,
But from the deep fountain within, which the touch causes to flow.
Joy gushes from the heart of Love, when Love is mutual and conscious.
   So too does the bitterness of Pain become more bitter,
When gall is poured into the wound by moral causes.
He who slips upon ice and breaks a limb,
He who with the sharp reaping-hook cuts his sinews unawares,
Has an agony of the body proportioned to the hurt.
But if the same wound were inflicted by ruthless malice,
By the wantonness of a strong youth, or by the tyranny of power;
The bitter sense of wrong might bring pain greater than the harm.
And if the doer were one beloved, as when a son wounds a mother,
Slight would be the body's anguish beside that of the heart.
   Therefore is the Tongue so sharp and terrible a weapon,
Dipped sometimes in a poison which may canker the soul.
For if he who assails with the tongue is our companion and intimate,
His unkindness may despoil us of homely and precious peace,
Fouling the wells of sympathy and marring society.
Or if the speaker be an enemy, full of calm malice,
Clever to choose for attack every sore place of our heart;

Then, unless we hate our sins more than the enemy can scorn them,
And are happily free from all innocent domestic calamity,
Who shall say what bitter agony his tongue may not cause us?
So intense are the pains and joys, which flow from our *moral* nature.

   Surely all the words which captivate the heart and ravish it,
Glory or Beauty and Power and Knowledge and Love and Virtue,
All, equally with the last, rise above the material or animal,
And cannot be estimated by animal pleasure.
Not mystical religion merely, but common sense, teaches,
That "the Moral is *beyond compare more worthy* than the Material;"
And that though things outward are fitly called good in themselves,
Yet their highest value is reached, when they minister to things inward.

   Upon this certainty, Religion founds a new Theorem,
That, "*In the mind of God*, the Moral is *the highest end* of the Material."
To this doctrine the soul gives assent by Intuition,
(Though no one can assay it by test of positive fact,)
Or because we know God to be pre-eminently Moral,
And see the loftier rank, which he gives to moral joys.
What else could be from *him*, who is Energy and Spirit and Life?—
Once more, and again, and again, consider this theorem:
Believe it not lightly, weigh it attentively:
The more you weigh it, the more it will seem true,
And necessary to be believed by all who know that God
Is a Spirit and is Moral and absolutely commands Virtue,
And causes it to abound with Peace and nameless Delight.
The dry or the impure heart may give but a feeble assent;
But according as each becomes pure and heavenly within,
In the same measure does this Theorem seem to become an Axiom.

   But *if* it be true, then on its basis is reared a Corollary,
High towering in reach, but strongly and broadly propped up,
That "Things Moral are *more lasting* than things Material."—
This also can never be verified by experience of fact,
For it stretches out above sight into the clouds of Faith:
Yet neither is it without reasonable argument and support.
For if the outer world is God's scaffold, and the inner world his building,
(Of which we are assured by the Theorem above approved,)
Surely the building must long outlast the scaffold.
Or to speak in plain terms and to dwell on the realities of life:—
When various endurance, perhaps calamitous,
With inward struggles toward light and higher virtue,
Has moulded man's heart into a purer temple of God;

If there be indeed a God who *intended* this process,
Who made light of all things outward,—of loss and of pain,—
Because of the high value which he set on man's Soul,
Which he would perfect in virtue by sacrificing all besides;
Is it credible that a result so dearly and elaborately bought
Was *intended* by him to perish with the fabric of the Body,
When it had barely attained its human perfection,
And was aspiring to a goodness more perfect and loftier?—
Such questions do not demonstrate; yet they convince the heart,
Perhaps in proportion to its childlike confidence in God.
Perhaps the minds which mistrust, are beset by some old error,
By materialistic philosophies and theories of Fate.
Be this as it may; the doctrine is at any rate probable,
To be received, till disproved, at least with respect.

From another quarter also confirmation is obtained.
The doctrine in question sprang out of Intuition,
And rests on direct argument, stronger or weaker.
But it might also have been proposed in guise of a *Hypothesis*,
Clearing up the dark points of God's moral Government,
By opening a field for future equitable redress.
It does not originate from the desire of solving that enigma;
Yet if it be admitted, it solves it satisfactorily,
Which is the appropriate duty of every Hypothesis.
If then, proposed as a mere Hypothesis, it might have plausibility,
This gives it a new strength, when it stands on other grounds.

See finally what is meant, when we abominate Materialism:
We mean not a metaphysical but a moral error;—
The error of valuing things Material above things Moral,
Choosing the reverse of God's mind, worse than by any sin of passion.
This is the essence of Mammon, and most confirmed unrighteousness.

IMMORTALITY OF GOD'S BELOVED.

Those who feel how far the Moral is better than the Material,
Find it hard to believe that true virtue can ever perish.
That which has God's nature seems to them immortal as God;
A noble sentiment, having nothing superstitious,
Nothing of mere fantasy and superficial credulity,
But springing up assuredly out of spiritual depths.

And as Love is the noblest and best of the affections,
So eminent in glory, that we pronounce it Divine,
The poet is praised, who denies that Love can die.
　But when those who stand over the grave of a virtuous friend
Lose faith in immortality, they grieve and lament,
Not merely that their friend loses happiness, or they their friend,
(For in every case they lose him,) but, that Virtue should perish,
That the Estimable and Lovely should exist no more.
This is no fond selfishness or foolish grief,
If that is lost to existence, which is of all things most valuable.
Rather, we could not be virtuous, if we did not grieve;
And if death is to be eternal, why not also grief?
　But if Virtue grieves thus for lost Virtue justly,
How then must God, the fountain of virtue, feel?
If our highest feelings, and the feelings of all the holy,
Guide rightly to the Divine heart, then it would grieve likewise
And grieve eternally, if Goodness perish eternally.
Nay, and as a man who should live ten thousand years,
Sustained miraculously amid perishing generations,
Would sorrow perpetually in the perpetual loss of friends;
And in foresight of their death, his affections would be blighted,
From fear to love too much those whom he cannot keep;
And as he would thus become callous and worn out in love,
In spite of benevolence and wise experience;
Even so, (some might judge,) the Divine heart likewise
Would stint its affections towards the creatures of a day,
And shun to love too much, lest it encounter grief.
Would it not be a yawning gulf of ever-increasing sorrow,
Losing every loved one, just when virtue was ripening,
And foreseeing perpetual loss, friend after friend, for ever;
So that all their training perishes, and has to be begun anew,
Winning new souls to virtue, to be lost as soon as won?
If then we must not doubt that the Highest has deep love for the holy,
Such love as man has for man, in pure and sacred friendship,
We seem justly to infer, that those whom God loves are deathless;
Else would the Divine Blessedness be imperfect and impaired.
　Nor avails it to reply by resting on God's Infinitude,
Which easily supports sorrow that would weigh down us:
For if to promote Virtue be the highest end with the Creator,
Then to lose his own work, not casually and by exception,
But necessarily and always, agrees not with his Infinitude,

More than his Wisdom, nor more than with his Blessedness.
In short, close friendship between the Eternal and the Perishing
Appears unseemly to the nature of the Eternal,
Whom it befits to keep his beloved, or not to love at all.
Whomsoever therefore he loves, they partake of his eternity;
But to say that he loves no man, is to make religion vain.
Hence it is judged, that "whatsoever God loveth, liveth with God,"
Whatsoever imbibes his essence and breathes his purity,
Whatsoever dwells in his bosom and rejoices in his nearness.

THE INFINITUDE OF THE FINITE.

It was taught of old, that whatever was born will die,
That whatever had a beginning will have an end,
That the Finite cannot give birth to the Infinite;
Hence, that nothing can be eternal in the ages to come,
Save what was eternal in the ages that are past.
If this be true, assuredly no after-life can concern us.
For, allowing to Plato the past eternity of our souls,
Yet, if our future soul be no more to us than the past soul,
Estranged from our consciousness, ignorant of its own identity,
No interest could we take in this future being,
As we take none in the self which preceded our birth:
And as no man would then conceive his future soul to be himself,
So neither would he care for the futurity of other men,
Or recognize God's Government in the continuity of souls.—
But let us more closely inquire into the ground of these Principles.
Every action of matter, we are told, has endless sequences.
For the first effect becomes cause of a second, the second of a third,
Nor can there be cessation to this ever-continued series.
If one solar planet were suddenly blotted out by miracle,
For ever would the future history of our system be altered.
Nay, if for an instant the attraction of one planet were doubled,
That also would leave upon all the system an eternal impress.
Thus finite action naturally bequeaths unending results.
Hereto the man of science may add, as caution and protest,
That each action of matter springs also from eternal causation,
For the series of causes backward is endless, as of effects forward.
Hence the future infinitude, while seeming to result from the finite,

Results as truly from the infinitude which is past.

From this we dissent not, nor venture upon controversy,
Dark and mysterious as is the thought of a *past eternity*,
Seemingly self-contrarious: but if there be Freedom of Will,
(Without which there is nothing Moral, and of course no Religion,)
Each moral agent acts of himself, and *not* as decreed by the past,
Yet by his free act initiates a series of effects unending,
And though finite Himself, generates Infinitude by every act.
Though new-born, he affects an eternity to come,
Propagating into endless ages onward many a result,
Which is not determined by the mysterious ages backward.

This peculiarity of Free Agents undermines the hypothesis,
That *all* infinity in the future demands infinity in the past;
And it teaches us the danger of assumptions thus abstract and unproved.
Also by immortality we mean not a divine state *extra-temporal*,
But an upholding of life through a long-linked train of times.
That nothing can be divine in the future, which was not in the past divine,
We admit; but if the new-born, which lived not in the past,
May live twenty or a hundred years, why not also a thousand?
Why not a thousand more, and a million more, and so on indefinitely?
We grasp not, for a Hereafter, any absolute and complete Eternity,
But the perpetual addition of new and still new years:
Nor see we, how this is made absurd by a past non-existence.

Perhaps, through the intense belief of these Greek dogmas,
Received in connection with materialistic philosophy,
Is to be explained the repugnance of some men to Free Will,
Who on the altar of Fate sacrifice Morals and Religion,
Sometimes intending service to God as well as to Truth.
Lest therefore the Necessarian plead these dogmas against Free Will,
Let us ask, whether it is so certain, *even* in things material,
That the causes of birth are causes likewise of dissolution,
So that whatsoever is born carries in it the seeds of death.

To this question the Astronomer, I think will answer *No*.
For Laplace has taught him, that this complex of Sun and Planets,
Harmoniously related in a common celestial life,
Had a beginning, had a birth, came forth from a state less complex,
When the body of the sun spread loose beyond our planets,
Which did not yet exist, save as outskirts of the monstrous sun:
And that the outmost planets were born first, as embryo rings,
Cast off by the accelerating whirl, when the bulk shrank in cooling:
Then of every ill-balanced ring the particles were attracted into a ball,

And planet after planet was shaped in slow succession
Through times which, if numerable, yet are not imaginable.
Ask that Astronomer who most surely believes this doctrine,
Whether he finds in our system the germs of its own dissolution,
And whether aught forbids to believe in its future eternity.
He will reply, that his science has here no prediction:
For in casting the eye forward into time unbounded,
We know not into what Spaces our system may be carried,
Whether into regions intense of heat beyond compare,
Or perhaps into extreme cold, marring to our harmony;
Nor know we within what new attractions it may come.
And as comets that range into far space are dissipated,
None can say, but that planets might be torn away from the sun,
Or the whole system swallowed in some foreign vortex.
But even if such a catastrophe be not impossible,
Yet it comes not to the system from within, but from forces extraneous.
And as, for a healthy man to be slain by violence from without,
Differs from the natural death of inward decay;
So too the Solar System, if liable to ruin from without,
Yet is not thereby a type of Death necessitated by Birth.
Viewed from within alone, it may be judged immortal;
So perfect is the balance of stability already reached.
For it is a noble truth of astronomy, securely won,
That all inward derangements of our system are self-compensating.
And as our days, waxing onward from their wintry length,
Reach at last their summer term and begin to wane,
And waning, have also a goal of smallness,
Nor ever outstep the limit at either end;
So the trespasses of the planets, of what kind soever,
Are but periodic waverings within narrow limits;
Nor do errors accumulate into instability,
But the whole is from within self-balancing and stable,
Fitted for Eternity, though framed in Time.
This may or may not be wholly true; but nothing in it seems absurd.
Nothing in it is refutable by a general axiom of metaphysics.

If then, in that science which is chiefly perfect,
And which alone can assay to compute futurity,
" That the Born should be Deathless" does *not* seem absurd,
Even in things without the higher life, without Free Will;
Necessarians surely have no pretext for confidence,
That whatever had a beginning must also have an end.

SOUL AND BODY.

That the Soul must die with the death of its organs,
Is more than mere Physiology can rightly pretend to know.
The inspector of brains and stomachs, in man and in brute,
By aid of eye and microscope and all the craft of chemistry,
Could never guess that man's brain *secreted Intelligence*
(As runs the phrase of some physicians) or possessed Free Will;
Nay, or that Man is wiser and nobler than the Ape.
By consciousness and morals this is known to us, not by anatomy.
The grand and glorious science which studies organic forces,
Sweeping into its wide drag-net life's humblest simplest forms,
Is blind to that moral life which lurks in the body unseen;
Nor does comparison of the lowest reveal the powers of the highest.
Free Will is moral life, unknown to the brute, (as we judge,)
And on Free Will alone rest the pleas of immortality.
No reasonings from the brutes touch this question at all,
Which soars altogether above the sphere of the physiologist.
His science teaches not, even that Man thinks and judges;
Much less, what Mechanism is for ever needful to Thought,
What is the Soul, what its growth, what its earning of force,
Or its necessary eternal dependence on its organs.
 By the Mother's circulating juices the Unborn Babe is fed,
And will die presently if that supply be cut off:
At length it is parted from its vegetative source,
And, losing its old supplies, gains a life higher than vegetative,
With an independence which might have seemed eternally impossible.
What then if the Body be a nurturing *mother* to the Soul,
Which depends on the body at first for vegetative and vital forces,
Until Death bursts the bands of union and sends the soul free,
Into a life higher than its parent's, and sustained without the parent's;
An independence which some call eternally impossible?
Then Death were a Birth, a birth into the world of souls.
This may be vain hypothesis, unsupported fantasy;
But its confutation belongs not to the domain of the physiologist,
Who cannot claim to know on what the spiritual powers depend.
 Thus the question of a Hereafter comes to us fresh and untouched,
Clear from all rightful pre-judgment by investigators of the body,
Open to the thoughtful auguries which religious instincts suggest.
If religious and moral science prove unable to decide this question,
Yet will they for ever legitimately discuss it.

Nor is the discussion useless, though no positive Certainty be reached:
For the conscience is enlivened by the very possibility of a Hereafter,
And man would not be man, if he did not meditate upon it,
Gazing into heaven's black depths, flooding his soul with homage
Toward *him* whose darkest wisdom claims ever reverential wonder.

WORTH OF THE SOUL.

Some are convinced by metaphysics, by physics and by authority,
That the soul of man is immortal, and *therefore* valuable.
Let the argument avail, with whomsoever it can avail,
But it is not that which we venture here to adopt.
A bad thing, if immortal, does not thereby gain worth,
Though a good thing is of greater worth by reason of duration,
Chiefly if with time it promise nobler growth.
But our reasoning has been contrariwise, that *if* the soul be worthy,
If it deserve to live, *then* it may have hope of life;
And desert is measured by capacity of improvement.
Thus we say not, "because immortal, therefore valuable,"
But rather, "because valuable, therefore immortal."
Some of the old Greeks believed, that virtue culminates
While the body is in middle age, and then declines;
And that to be peevish, selfish, cowardly, covetous,
With other vices, grows necessarily on old age,
Which in its normal state encounters loss of virtue.
If this were true, it would indeed be a weighty fact,
Nor could there be stronger disproof of man's immortality.
Then man would be like to the brute, shut into narrow limits,
Nor for soul, more than for body, could longer life be desired.
But the opinion is overstrained, and on several grounds unjust,
Partly because decay of sense closes the avenues of information,
Giving the appearance of selfishness even to the unselfish;
Partly from judging wrongly *who* is the normal man:—
Not one diseased in body and morbid in spirits,
Not one who is pampered by honour and high observance,
Not one who has not made virtue his chief pursuit.
Few indeed are the men who can be fitly judged normal,
So as to found hereupon proof that virtue declines:

WORTH OF THE SOUL.

Nor is any reasoning from *averages* here appropriate.
Rather, if there be *any* (as we know that there are in truth)
In whom years and decay set no limit to goodness,
It must be judged that this is the state really normal,
And that the human soul has no natural limit to virtue.
   Truly all life is higher than the lifeless,
And whatever can love is better than the loveless.
How could a vast mass of matter, as the inanimate Moon,
Compare in value with one warm human heart,
In the estimate of him whose Spirit is our life?
To think, and to love,—oh how godlike is each faculty!
They are our birthright, our nature; let us not disparage them,
Nor admit the charge, that it is human self-flattery
To estimate highly the human soul.
Except God himself, we know nothing to compare to it.
Creatures there may be, and probable are, higher than we;
(For who will dream that Man exhausts spiritual Creation?)
But only through Life and Love can they be higher,
And in a smaller degree their glory is our glory.
Let not then our *littleness* induce an unwise humility,
Because we are but as dust in an infinite universe:
Nor suppose that he, to whom *every* thing finite is small,
Is too great for our littleness, or can despise it.

ANIMAL DEVELOPMENT.

   The things in which Man and Brute agree are many,
The one point in which Man and Brute differ is mighty;
And through comparison and contrast opposite judgments result.
In the body and in the animal life the likeness is all but sameness;
Our passions and emotions and affections are greatly like theirs;
Yet man is self-guiding and moral and improvable,
And able to discern God, able to aspire to him;
None of which things can we discover in the brute.
Now whereas many persons have brought proofs of immortality,
Which applied to beasts equally as to man,—
Proofs drawn from mere life and motion and immaterial thought,—
A few have been willing to extend immortality to the brutes;
But the majority, unable to believe that shell-fish and insects

And microscopic animalcules were destined to immortality,
Have held, that for reasonable belief of a human Hereafter
It is needful to keep asunder the case of man and of beast.
Let us not here undertake to dogmatize against the brutes:
Nevertheless it is certain that they do not fall within the arguments
On which alone we have based the hopes of a hereafter for man.
Yet neither may we overlook the pleas of our common animal-origin.

    Geologists and Astronomers convince us that our Earth was once
A ball of fiery liquid, a sea of melted rock,
Which in the course of vast ages was chilled slowly,
Until a crust curdled around it, like to ice upon water,
Which, often perhaps melted and re-made, at length became settled,
And long remained hot; but when in longer time it cooled,
And the crust thickened, and the inner ball shrank,
Then cracks and shrivellings ran over the whole surface,
And some parts fell in, and others were thrust upward,
And beds were made for the oceans, and mountains appeared,
While, by new composition of elements, Sea and Air were made.
Before that time no living creatures could be,—
Such creatures as live by breath and are killed by fierce heat:
They all therefore came upon the earth at a distant but finite time
By the will and wisdom of God and by his creative forces.

    Yet of God's action we know nothing that could liken him to man,
Or liken his creation to our manual workmanship.
All his dealing, as known to us, is as a Law and as a Life,
Ever constant, ever like itself, as befits the Unchangeable.
And the progress of Science has persuaded pious philosophers
That the Highest *creates*, as he *maintains*, by eternal forces,
By an unceasing law, by an ever-acting energy,
Not by a rare or solitary effort of irregular power.
And the vast series of diverse creatures, seen in Geology,
Is explained by Geologists as so many successive evolutions,
Brought forth by a divine law, unknown to us, yet undoubted.
Nor only so; but it is further taught, as a tenet inevitable,
That the *first* created organisms, of the simplest rudest class,
Must have clustered into life out of things unorganized,
Whether by electric and cohesive or by other Divine forces,
When first the raw Earth became fit for organic life.
What else could any one reasonably mean by their *Creation?*
Yet this Creation was but a Birth, or a Growth special of kind,
If no class of organisms, vegetable or animal

Was made, save of material pre-existing on the earth;
Whether out of the unorganic, or the more complex out of the simpler.
   If so much as this be true, very many minds at once
Will push to results beyond, from which the learned still shrink.
For if all Creation was but an outburst of Divine Law,
Through which the material here present blossomed into life,
Displaying the divine Soul which worked through the brute Matter;
Not only may it seem that Creation is a Birth or Growth,
But that those successive species, testified in geology,
Continuous in time, were also continuous in causation,
Each new arising race being children of an earlier race,
Changed with the change of elements, and ever advancing,
In such long years as only the Eternal can afford;
Till from the dwellers in the seas and from the meanest insects
Rose reptiles and birds and beasts four-footed.
And moreover, if *other* creations were by Law,
Unfolded of germs which gathered up old materials;
Hardly would the Creator, whose methods we judge to be unchanging,
Follow a contrary method in the creation of Man:
Especially when it is noted, how the human frame is modelled,
Bone after bone corresponding to bones of beast and bird;
Beside other harmonies, set forth by physiologists,
Which prove to the unbiassed a strict community of development.
Many therefore will infer, that the earliest tribes of Man
Grew out of, or were born out of, some creatures lower than Man;
We mean not out of existing apes, nor care to say out of what.
But if our race had a beginning and grew out of something,
And existing brutes had a beginning and grew out of something,
(The earlier something being in each case doubtless inferior,)
While the frames of man and brute denote close relations of origin;
To many minds (I say) no *historical chasm* is credible,
But they believe that the Human is a growth out of the non-Human,
A growth by continuous operation, by gradual and slow action,
Whether the final transition was, or was not, abrupt.
To such an opinion unbiassed thought leads some men,
While seeking solely for truth by legitimate methods.
   But the conclusion is thought by many fatal to immortality;
If possibly there were once races between human and brutal,
Too good to be mortal, too base for immortality.
But I see not how this is weightier than the fact of present Idiots,
Nay, or more than the case of children who die in Infancy,

To whom none of the moral arguments for a Hereafter can apply,
When no Conscience has been formed, and no Free Will has been possible.
Yet with them surely transition is gradual, states are intermediate,
Nor can our philosophy pretend to draw sharp divisions:
Theists to whom this is no difficulty, need find none in the other.
But let us consider more generally this doctrine of transition.

 Is it forgotten, that effects, though under a Continuous Cause,
Are often at certain stages abrupt and even convulsive,
With a gap between the old and new which we call Discontinuous?
As when slowly increasing cold may fall upon wintry water,
Which at first becomes lighter, yet is water still.
Liquid and refreshing, diluting and purifying;
Until by further cooling it suddenly shoots forth crystals,
And water becomes ice and the liquid solid rock,
Which no longer can flow down the throat nor wash the body,
And which none might ever guess to have been liquid.
Or again, in every animal birth, when an embryo leaves the mother,
How sudden is the transition from darkness into light,
From vegetative growth to spontaneous active life!
The Causes were continuous, the Result is discontinuous.
And so deep is this seated in the simplest laws of action,
That those whose Calculus traces the issues of such laws,
Know that when the Generator is continuous, often the Generated is abrupt,
And the infinitesimal of the Hypothesis breeds the finite of the Conclusion;
So that gaps impassable arise where least expected,
And smooth curves bristle with Peaks and loose Branches gather into an oval,
And lines of brilliancy flash forth amid the unbrilliant.
Yea, and sometimes where Nature is healthiest, this abruptness is sharpest:
As when a healthy man, wearied healthily with healthful toil,
Sinks suddenly into sleep, and becomes a mere animal,
Void of self-guidance, void of Conscience, deaf to the voice of God,
Irrational and fatuous, carried into dreaming vanities,
And, during his sleep, no better than his dog or his horse.
Then, recruited by the brain's idleness, he wakes abruptly,
And starts suddenly up fresh for the toils of life,
Strong in brain, strong in sinew, and a worshipper of God once more:
So sudden is the change from fatuity to reason during health.
But if the mind be overworked or the body be unhealthy,
No longer is the passage from sleep to waking so abrupt.
But he, who is fain to sleep, for a long time cannot sleep,
And slumber comes on him piecemeal, limb after limb.

His lower limbs and his hands are in a doze before his brain,
Nor perhaps do all the faculties of his mind rest at once,
But they are partially benumbed and partially active.
And in this abnormal sleep Visions are possible,
Being dreams streaked with intelligence or glowing with religion,
When Conscience and Reason blend fitfully with Silliness.
And when in the morning he would wake, he cannot wake all at once;
Self-remembrance revives, but his limbs are heavy,
Nor when his mind is wholly returned, does his body yet obey.
May we not rather compare to this the state of the Insane and of the Idiot.
These are deviations from health, like the sleep of the mesmeric,
A morbid intermediate condition, not a normal one.
Who shall say, but that in the real history of the human origin,
(Which was normal, we presume, and natural, not unhealthy,)
Man, though rising from Not-Man, came forth sharply defined,
As when we start suddenly into reason out of healthy sleep?
Nor need we trouble ourselves with a theory of Idiotic Races,
When nothing in our Science nor in our Hypotheses demands a belief in them.
   Return we then to the problem of Moral Beings as we find it.
Between moral man and unmoral brute the gulf is real;
And if the Future of each is to be generated out of its Present,
The gulf which exists may be destined to grow wider,
The brute shrinking into nothingness, the man spreading through infinitude.
If the brute is incapable of making progress toward God,
Why should he live, unimproving, in an improving world?
And if the man is able to rise according to the Eternal counsels,
Why may not he grow for ever, in life grafted upon life?
Be this true or false, is not the present question:
Only it is not disproved by the doctrine of Animal Development.

BROTHERHOOD OF MEN.

   Fellow countrymen are not loved barely because born on the same land:
Sometimes even the same land rears bitter enemies;
As when two hostile races dwell side by side, or intermixed,
As Philistines with Hebrews, Pelasgians with Hellenes,
Saxons and Normans on the soil of Britain,
Or even as might have been French and English in Canada.
When neighbourhood invites wrong, with border-war and ravage,

Between those who are not coupled in equal and approved law,
A common soil is to rude men but a bond of enmity.
It is never the Material, but only the Moral, that unites men,
Though the Moral can only act through the form of the Material.
　Even with the same nation, the same language, same laws and religion,
And where common patriotism has joined men against the foreigner,
Primitive social inequalities unduly sundering ranks
Put enmity between High and Low and cause implacable strife;
As in the cities of ancient Greece, or of Italy in the middle age,
Where bitter feuds made civil war ordinary and deadly.
Deem not then that true brotherhood in any spiritual sense
Can come to mankind from a mere material connection.
　Why are brotherhood and sisterhood proverbial of attachment?
Not solely from the naked fact of common parentage,
But because the fact is blended with plentiful moral meaning.
If the same mother watched over their helpless infancy;
If the same parents loved them all, and taught them mutual love;
If the same father provided for them and trained them and counselled them,
With equal anxiety seeking the welfare of all;
If in infancy and childhood and in rising youth they were companions,
Giving and receiving sweet pleasure and tender comfort
By mutual self-denial and mutual aid
Through kindness of the elder and compliance of the younger;
These, and other such things, are the true bond of affection,
Making *brother* and *sister* dear names, hard to parallel on earth.
　But if Plato's Commonwealth could be made a reality,
And no mother reared her own child, and family life were destroyed,
And children were sorted by ages and brought up in troops,
And no tender remembrances united brothers and sisters
From common parental love nor from old companionship;
Surely the bare fact of being progeny from the same womb
Would never avail to cause love or mutual care.
　So neither has the belief of a descent from Adam and Eve
Hindered the dire atrocities of human race against race.
Nor will it ever hinder: but those who want an excuse,
When resolved to treat fellow-men as cattle, but more cruelly,
Persuade themselves that these are born from some Cain or some Amalek
Or from Canaan, cursed by God to unending slavery.
Not the belief about Adam and Eve, but union in a common faith
Has hitherto had chief force to bridle avarice and insolence.
Moslem acknowledges the brotherhood of Moslem, and Christian of Christian,

And the priests of each feel enslavement of their brethren scandalous.
   Herein is wrapped up the true meaning of Human Brotherhood.
Men are men and are not brutes,—not because sons of one Adam,
But because sons of one God who dwells in all consciences.
In the childhood of Paganism, in the manhood of Monotheism,
One Parent watches over their childhood or supports their manhood,
And commands their virtue, and rears them to sympathy,
And puts them under common law, with like reward or punishment,
As brethren of one family, citizens of one country.
Two things complete the definition of Man:
"A *Body* which may be parent to a race mixed with ours,
A *Mind* capable of Free Will, and thereby of Morality and Religion."
   But the moral rights of mankind spring from their moral side only,
And are not concerned in questions of the body at all.
If Black and White races could have no common progeny,
If their forms were as unlike as the horse and the deer,
Yet both were subjected to the same law of Conscience,
With the same loves and hatreds, the same pains and joys;
The same law of right and wrong would rule over both,
Virtue be their common requirement, and Freedom be essential to Virtue,
Nor ever could it be endurable that the one be chattels of the other.
By the unchangeable law of the Highest, let man struggle as he may,
Curse comes upon the nation which tramples its brethren down.
And let none dream, that, by measuring men's bones and studying old pictures,
And arguing for many origins of our various-tinted tribes,
He can turn those into cattle who have the minds and hearts of men,
Or deny brotherhood to those in whom God is a moral energy,
Speaking to them by conscience, if haply they may seek him.
Surely he is their Father, and they our true brothers and sisters,
Though Abraham, Noah, Adam alike disown the progeny.

THE ALTERNATIVES.

Let us resume in mind the broad theories of the Infinite.
Pantheism may be inattentive to the facts of the human Conscience;
But Atheism shuts its eyes to the wide phenomena of the world,
And is untenable to general good-sense for a single moment,
While denying that a Higher Mind is visible in the universe.
Let us set this aside; then Pantheism and Theism remain.

The Pantheist, discerning a Creative and Moulding Spirit,
Which animates and guides and perfects the universe,
May possibly yet doubt whether that Spirit is *moral:*
This is the baser and worse phase of Pantheism.
But others, while believing the Creative Spirit to be moral,
So as to design that man shall be perfected through Virtue;
Yet suppose him too great to pay attention to *individuals;*
Or to care for the destruction of any one man's virtue.
And manifest facts, they think, confirm this judgment;
Since we see how often the promise of virtue is blighted,
As buds by the east wind, piteously and fatally;
Yet new virtue sprouts up and blooms into flower and fruit,
Accomplishing the will of the Eternal, and glorifying man.
Thus, acting by general laws, for general perfection,
Remote from created minds abides the Infinite one,
Unapproachable by man's sorrow or desire or hope,
Negligent alike of our worship and of our prayer,
Nay, neither smiling on devotion nor frowning on sin,
But satisfied that, *on the Average*, virtue advances.
Thus his Government looks solely to the progress of a *system*,
Sacrificing individuals for the whole without regret,
As a captain of war devotes thousands to win a petty post,
And wades to his victory through the blood of his own bravest.
And as God is to the universe the source of life and health,
But also to individuals the source of disease and death;
So God is then to the universe the spring and centre of virtue,
But not the more a succour to the virtue of any one man,
Or a fit object of Trust to virtue in its struggles.
Thus Pantheism cuts the bond between virtue and religion,
And like Paganism, gravitates easily into the immoral,
Enervating or congealing the desolated soul.
The love of man to God becomes unseemly or impossible,
And praise of God is but admiration of the Unlistening,
And stops short in chill wonder at inobservant Infinitude.
In short, to the Pantheist God is only *outside* the heart,
Nor can it be otherwise, while *God in Conscience* is overlooked.

But the Theist, finding God to speak in each Conscience separately,
Cannot believe that he is inobservant of *individual* conduct:
Here it is that he cardinally separates from the Pantheist.
Between these alternatives thoughtful men must take their choice.
And the question is not, which of two Religions is better,

But whether heart-devotion to the Highest is an intrinsic absurdity.
For where direct sympathy between God and each soul is severed,
As by the Pantheist,—there is speculation, admiration, awe,
But not faith, love, worship; and therefore no other religion,
Than that unconscious devotion which is possible even to an Atheist.

FUTURE OF THE RIGHTEOUS.

"Vanity of vanities, all is vanity,"
Cried to ancient Israel the preacher sated with pleasures.
"All men come to one end, be their life what it may:
As dieth the fool, so dieth the wise man;
A living dog is better than a dead lion."
Such is the voice of the grave to the outward ear;
The testimony of sense can teach nothing of immortality.
When the animal body dies, the animal life is extinct,
And the student of the body discovers nothing of soul.
Yet, plain as are the facts, and obvious the reasonings,
By which outward sense awards the soul to the grave,
The inward sense of mankind consent not to that award,
But with spiritual growth hitherto forebodes a future.
Much has above been written, addressed to this aim,
Yet it is not amiss here to sum up the arguments,*
Which vindicate our foreboding as neither weak nor fanciful.
It springs not from fond vanity and arrogant folly,
From exaggerated flattery and idolizing of self.
It is not the selfish heart, nor the conceited and presumptuous,
The flighty and ambitious, which most believes in immortality.
And if we set self aside, looking solely at others,
Our auguries of a future remain not less firm:
Yea, still more clearly does then Faith inly prophesy
Life continued to the pure and holy, to the lovers of God.
For the extinction of the righteous screams discord to Faith,
To which otherwise holy truth sounds as melody.
Even when the arguments for a Hereafter rise out of the personal,
Yet in no case are they ever confined to the personal,
Nor savour of selfishness and overweening folly.

---

* Most of these are stated with much beauty and force in Mr. Sutton's eccentric book 'Quinquenergia.'

If the human soul have an early limit of perfection,
If it have no element of infinitude, more than has the body,
But attains a zenith, and thereupon naturally declines;
Then vainly would you augur for it any longer life.
Nor would it avail to demand for it a scene of redress,
Great as might be the wrongs here innocently endured,
If the man, like the brute, were unfitted for higher progress.
But every human instinct and sentiment denies this;
And religion pre-eminently opens infinite aspirations,
Which, since God is truthful, cannot be normally delusive,
But command our assent, until error is detected in them.
Atheism is consistent, in denying both God and his teaching:
Pantheism can forebode at most but an improvement in our *race*:
But Theism, which claims a divine watchfulness over *individuals*,
Ill admits that a living coward is better off than a dead martyr,
Or that bold obedience to God can ever be an imprudence.
Hence, whatever arguments avail to establish pure Theism,
Resist also the belief that a holy soul can perish,
Unless its holiness decay naturally with the body.
Far opposite appears the fact, and opposite is the augury,
Which we draw from the sufferers by undeserved disease,
Who grow up into virtue and meek joy amid sorrow,
Yet perish prematurely with their frail body,
After countless pains, and after attaining a high goodness.
For it is hard to opine, that the great Teacher trained such a soul,
Through so costly a perfecting, to perish for ever.

But in fact, the same reasoning may be applied more widely.
To believe in God and to serve him, is to become a vassal of the Highest,
To be guided by his Spirit, to be made a work of his moulding,
To be joined to him by vows and worship, by thanksgiving and holy joy.
Scarcely will one convince the soul, which God draws alway higher,
That when closest to his life, it is mounting into death.
It has learnt well, that Virtue is the highest end of existence,
That "the aim of Creation is the perfecting of souls,"
That God must cherish Virtue, as the most precious of products,
And therefore, cannot be indifferent to its perishing:
And that to lose those he loves, is to lose his own work,
Against his own blessedness and against his own wisdom.
Can then the friends of the Eternal be parted from his love?

All the world is a battle-field: and is its carnage for nothing?
What end does the All-ruling work out by its toils?

Not mere energy, not mechanism, not outward wellbeing;
But everywhere are the wise of heart pressed onward to believe,
That things outward are the scaffold, and Souls the true building.
Every day we feel and we know and we avow
That nothing but mind and soul gives value to things material.
Surely then (cry the devout) this world is but a workshop of Soul:
"The seen is but temporal, the unseen is eternal."
    What is True is always Best: then what is Best is always True.
Where truth is known to us directly, we accept it, and believe it to be best.
Where truth is otherwise unknown, but what *appears** to be best is discerned,
Then, until more directly taught, we presume that best to be true.
What the Hereafter may be, and where, how, when,—we know not;
Every attempt to picture it to the mind, is futile, perhaps hurtful,
Warning us hereby, that no definite anticipations can be healthful to us:
Yet to believe *some* Hereafter for the good, confirms our noblest thoughts.
Who knows but that as yet we are in the mere infancy of religion,
And that in happier times, when collective mankind is holier,
Purer insight may be man's general endowment, and our dim auguries may be
        deemed certainties?

FUTURE OF THE WICKED.

    Some teach that the wicked will hereafter be condemned
And punished in flames that are not purifying,
Flames that harden sin and make it inveterate,
Evergrowing and unconquerable, unto endless despair;
Flames preservative of life and torment, of curses and hatred.
    Never let me believe a frightful dream, deadly to piety,
A Pagan monstrosity made worse than in Pagan fable,
A horror which no proof imaginable could make credible;
Which hardens man's heart, if we believe such a gospel,

---

    * To decide what will be Best, is too high for the human mind, where the number of possibilities is infinite; but not always too high, where we have to select between Yes and No. Thus, 1. The power in Nature is either intelligent or not intelligent; 2. God either is or is not attentive to human adoration; 3. God either does or does not watch over the interests of his self devoting servants; 4. There either is a future life for some of mankind, or there is no future for any.—In each of these four statements there is no third possibility; and in none of the four cases is it difficult to decide which alternative is absolutely more desirable, or which alternative it does us more good to believe.

Overthrows God's justice, if he punish the finite by infinitude,
Overthrows his government and providential sovereignty,
If he cannot help Sin from being eternal and ever worse;
Overthrows his goodness, foresight and wisdom,
By making our creation a blunder infinite and inexcusable.
This Pagan horror is still taught in public creeds,
Is still believed by the coarse-minded or ill-trained,
But is practically renounced by the tender-minded and thoughtful.

But others have taught a doctrine which allures the heart;
That the wicked, as the righteous, are destined to longer life;
But by constraints and discipline, by new trial in new scenes,
Shall there be trained to the virtue, which here they despised,
Thus through heavenly mercy, in spite of present failure,
Even these at length are joined to the blessed family of the good.

Oh, never let me deny this! never let me stint the mercy
Of that august loveliness whose holy goodness we adore!
Who shall fathom his purposes, his wise condescension,
Or know what hearts are incurable to his remedies?
How great were the joy in heaven, how wondrous the ecstasy,
If this dream of our delirious longings should ever prove sober truth!
God's realities surpass our fancies; he may fulfil where we despair:
And what all must desire, who love God and goodness,
Seems to come as a revelation and as a glorious foreshadowing.
This hope let us cherish, if haply the most High fulfil it.

Yet, hanging over depths unfathomed, peering into the Allwise heart,
To ponder with thoughtful faith over mysteries unopened,
It is wiser to speak with reserve and with lowly utterance,
Reflecting on human narrowness and on our own misjudgments,
How often God's Government disappoints our auguries,
And how the Free Will of sinners resists his ordinance.
The green twig may be trained aright; but what of the gnarled trunk?
The limits of God's patience we know not: one thing we know:
His world is made to advance, and *none incorrigible shall abide in it.*
How can Sin strike firm roots in the garden of the Holy One,
The All-mighty, the All-cultivator, to whom the Universe is an Eden,
A glory and a pleasantness? who delighteth in his Creation,
And blesseth and governeth and consecrateth the whole.
The fire of his Spirit all-pervading must either melt or destroy.

Neither may we class the imperfect and unfortunate with the wicked.
Many are spoiled for virtue in this world, and cannot attain it,—
Flowers crushed in the bud, marred beyond recovery,

Whose inexperience the iniquity of others has deceived,
Or, it may be, enslaved from infancy, and made tools of crime.
Who shall divine how the most Merciful shall deal with these?
His counsels are now secret; but when at length they are manifest,
The voice of praise and adoration, the thrill of infinite delight,
Shall respond to his holy wisdom, in reverent applause.
If his judgments are severe, yet he fails not to be gracious:
And those whom we pity, he must pity; for, our hearts are narrower than his.
Whosoever can be saved, he will save; for Mercy inheres in Righteousness.

PREVENIENT GRACE.

He who is so blessed as to be conscious of loving God,
I deem, is doubly blessed in knowing that he is beloved in turn.
And never will such a one say: "I took the initiative in love:
"I discerned the beauty of the Highest; I courted and I wooed him;
"I caused him to reciprocate affection; I won him for my heart;
"And because I first loved him, therefore does he love me."
But the believer in God's love holds that love to be unchangeable,
And that as God loves to-day, so loved he yesterday;
Therefore his affection precedes that of man, and is "Prevenient;"
Therefore also must its eye glance beyond the present to the future.
And as a mother who contemplates her infant in the cradle,
Contemplates not only what it is, but what it is to be,
Filling her heart with fond anticipations, with joyful hopes;
And reckons that the child shall hereafter become wise and good,
And shall know its mother, and shall respond to her love,
And shall become accomplished man or woman, noble and worthy of love,
Even so, as in dim outshadowing, may we judge of the Divine heart,
And rightly believe that it loves for our promise, not for our desert;
Loves for that which we can be, for that which we are about to be,
For that which is now in germ, not for that only which has blossomed.
Unless we are conscious of this germ, this divine "potentiality,"
Never can we recognize a divine life within us,
Nor claim near relationship to the mighty Soul of Heaven.
But to be conscious of initial life, brings no vain conceit,
But rather much abashment that this life is so feeble,
Its promise so ill fulfilled, its action so fitful.
Also another wide contemplation here opens upon us.—

Primitively, in every man some seed of virtue was planted,
Unless he be but an idiot, insane, and no moral agent.
Whether by man's perversity this seed may be wholly marred,
Irrecoverably ruining the soul;—is open to assertion or denial.
If we assert it, there is a part of mankind justly reprobate,
Destined to perish as brutes, and not partaking of Divine Love;
Though hard indeed to say, even with trembling, is this.
Yet even so, while any one retains visible germs of goodness,—
I mean not wild gentleness, such as is even in fierce beasts,
But some power of *Conscience*, which sacrifices Self to *Duty*;—
So long the hope is reasonable, that an eye purer than ours
Looks complacently on that poor soul, and designs its perfection,
Loving it for its future, in spite of its doubtful present:
Nor may any one justly think, that those whose virtue does but struggle,
Whom passions and folly sway, are not (in the future) "God's true people,"
Are not now already his beloved, his children in the cradle,
Destined to a future reciprocation in his love.
 Oh, what love to man, even to fierce wild sinners,
Might haply our hearts maintain, if we believed that God loves them!
Then might we ourselves, imitating the Father in Heaven,
Put forth "Prevenient Grace," and love them in their baseness,
Divinely anticipating their future noble state.
Nor would this lead to weakness, and abolish severity:
For the same God, who is the symbol of our highest purest love,
Shrinks not from intense severity, in upholding his every law.
Justice is not opposed to Mercy, and much less to Goodness.

WATERS OF LETHE.

 Those who sang to ancient nations a fable of immortality,—
Poets, priests, sages,—taught, whether as fact or parable,
That the imperfect souls of men, who were destined to live anew,
Drank from a deep dark river the waters of forgetfulness,
And returned to the upper world as tender spirits of infants,
Purged from much sin by forgetting, and able to win new virtue.
 This was but a Pagan vision, painted when the heart and conscience
Was a mirror but rudely polished to reflect the thoughts of heaven:
'Twas a mere rash conjecture, earnestly retained by few.
Yet possibly this wild fancy, stript of its vain accompaniments,

May suggest, even to us, a contemplation not vain.
    To all imperfect natures a partial *forgetfulness* is useful.
It is not primarily by repentance that the sins of boyhood are purged,
But by change of circumstance and of habit, and by better contact.
The hardened youth, accustomed to self-justifying,
Measuring morals by his fellows, counting all " school offences " light,
Learns obedience on a new scene, hears of business or of science,
Or of " glory " and discipline, or is abashed by love.
Thus he is immersed in new hopes and fears, new duties and desires ;
Whence follow new habits, wiser thoughts, purer passions,
Until the whole mind is moulded into a new stamp.
As the Christian, when dipt under the water, rose up a new man,
And was taught to *forget* his past sins, done in the years of " God's winking,"
And Repentance was to him but Reform, not heart-rending remorse :
And so he came forth, as new-born, into a new world of virtue,
Forgetting his old self, and marked by a new name,
As though the font of his baptism had been the Lethe-water :
So haply may it be with all guilt that is puerile and barbaric,
Guilt of the ignorant, of the volatile, of the immature conscience,
Guilt incurred under evil pressure, without deep purpose.
And oh how large a part of human guilt are we naming !
Everywhere the many are well-intentioned, and only weak,
Unable to resist circumstances, and thus drawn into sin.
But where sin is from without, the cure may be from without,
And the soul in a new world may drop many an evil habit,
When the grave changes its relations, its associations, its memories.
    Even when guilt is more deliberate and deeply ingrained,
Change of exterior and new constraint may open a new door to virtue.
We are glad when the felon escapes from his net of crime,
Old customs and evil comrades, into a new world and new scenes.
He loses not identity, but is surely the same man,
Yet, by grace of heaven, he may now run a new career,
Especially if the memory of his old crimes be suppressed,
And none can whisper them against him, nor any old face recall them.
To such a man how precious is a draught of Lethe-water !
    None of us know,—only God knows,—whether Remorse follows such Reform !
Whether bitter misery and humiliation eat deep into the spirit,
After it has learned better ways and becomes self-conscious of the past.
But whatever misery of this kind may come as natural *retribution*,
We may well believe is also needful for *purifying*,
So that Divine love and severity never are at variance.

And if there be reserved a future to the very guiltiest,
Power, Love and Justice will still be seen in harmony,
Making sin bitter, only that sin may be destroyed.

THE DOUBTER.

There is a man, who doubts concerning human immortality.
He does not criticize our arguments, but he assails the conclusion.
For, he says, universal mankind *deserves* no immortality.
If by physical reasonings immortality can be established,
Then let it be established; but on moral grounds
None may award life immortal to the entire human race.
Why should barbarous man, stunted in soul and intellect,
Variously perverted and depraved, blind to all true religion,
Live beyond the grave, on religious and moral account,
More than the ape, dog, seal or elephant, unperverted natures?
Why should children who die in birth, or five minutes after birth,
More than the child that dies just before birth, inherit a second life?

But if you separate mankind, and say that some are to live again,
And that others, unsusceptible of growth, will not live again,
You separate man from his wife, friend also from friend,
Parents from children; and you violate affection.

Nor will any hypothesis avail to avoid painful results:
Many say, "Give me no immortality without my dearest ones:"
Others say, "To reunite ties broken by death and by diverse mental growth,
"Would be to me intolerable: I pray rather not to exist."
Nor are human characters so sharply cut apart into two classes,
That one is fitted for after-life, and the other is clearly unfit.

Of such objections no refutation can here be offered,
If they are weightier than the arguments above stated, they will outweigh those
But if the previous arguments are weightier, then those will outweigh these,
Until either of these or of those some direct refutation be found.

HISTORICAL WARNINGS.

Man's belief in a Future Life has its own history,
Which must not be overlooked and ought not to be misread.

HISTORICAL WARNINGS.

Some zealous Theists say that the belief is a tenet with all mankind,
A primary truth of Intuition, co-ordinate with Morals,
An aspiration of savage and of sage, cardinal to spiritual life,
Not less universal and cogent than a belief in God.
Yet the sobriety of Truth announces a different tale.

Even that ancient nation, chief depositary of Monotheism,
Channel of spirituality to all the peoples of Christendom,
Yet from the age of King David to the last King of David's line
Had no clear authoritative tenet concerning human immortality.
At most a Psalmist now and then, of date unknown,
Raised for his own soul an aspiration more or less confident.
But neither the sacerdotal creed nor the national religious sentiment
Rested upon or implied renewal of life after death.
Such doctrine (theologians affirm) was superseded
By a crude misinterpretation of present Divine judgment,
As dealing prosperity to the righteous, misery to the evil doer.
Even now, if report errs not, vast millions of our race,
Reared in the Buddhist creed, are apathetic to immortal hopes.
Nay, who is there among us, that to the neglected millions of Europe
Ascribes intuitional yearnings that aspire to future life?
The modern belief on this topic first appears among Hebrews,
When, dismayed by the failure of Divine succour against foes,
They saw their royalty sink under the stranger's rude violence.
Missing Retribution here, they looked for it in a world to come.
—Such origin of the tenet is not wholly commendatory.

Nor is every form of the doctrine beneficent in tendency.
Unintellectual barbarians, vehement and noble-hearted,
Believing this doctrine, are prodigal of life,
And for company in the unseen world massacre both beasts and men.
Ancient Thrace and Scythia, modern Mexico and Florida,
Dahomey and Thibet, testify of frightful bloodshed,
—For vain glory or wild fancy—prompted by belief in immortality.
Many have been braver in battle, some over their chieftain's grave
Themselves have slain themselves, for companionship in the Spirit-land.
In a certain French crusade,—(the tale is well known in history)—
Through this very belief indiscriminate massacre was perpetrated.
"Slay all!" said the Bishop: "heretics or faithful, matters not:
"God, in his Day of Judgment, will himself distinguish his own."
To an earnest believer, in the splendour of immortal bliss
This human life pales and is counted but as dross.
In comparison to the glory which must hereafter be revealed,

What even is present agony, and the terror of violent death?
Thus life is esteemed cheap, and human misery of no account,
And the saint has become stonyhearted, nay, cruel as a tiger.
   To teach that a future life is mere bliss and glory,
Whether to some or to all, is surely then evil in tendency,
As it is evil tenfold to believe Sin and Misery eternal.
To undervalue this life cannot be wise nor healthful:
Our duties are in it. To Man's future on this earth
No limit of time is set by nature or reason:
Here is our obvious work, fertile of good incalculable.
Ought not unselfish affections to be fixed on things human,
If their goal be divine? No argument suggests,
That for finite creatures future life can be without a task,
Without progress, without pain, without hope or fear.
No doctrine concerning the future can ever be so sure,
As we are sure that the Present life is God's invaluable gift.

MODERN POLYTHEISM.

   Pantheism and Polytheism are twin sisters,
Born from dreamy Poetry and unmoral Philosophy;
And as is their parents', such is their moral temperament,
Ever verging to the immoral, and void of stability.
Even under monotheistic creeds, in minds poetic or mystical,
No sooner does morality become corrupt or confused,
Than Polytheism or Pantheism will presently reappear.
So has the Christian creed, cumbered by saint-worship,
Degenerated for ages into a new Polytheism.
So also again may the germ of the same thing be seen,
When men think to commune with the spirits of the dead;
As the great historical[*] critic, who, in his second wife's travail,
Implored the spirit of his first wife to soften her pains.
Such communing leads everywhere headlong into prayer:
The prayer is idolatrous, and a real polytheism,
That dulls religion's energy and makes its depths shallow,
Harmful therefore to morals and offensive to piety.
   He who ascribes to the deceased a power so divine,
That they can be present at pleasure, roaming through the universe,
And can hear words addressed to them, by day or by night;

---

[*] Barthold Niebuhr.

Has so overstept the limits of sober reason,
That he knows not what other high power he may not attribute.
Hence he fancies, "*Perhaps* they may be able to fulfil my wishes:
If I may make entreaty to my living friend, why not to my deceased?
Be he in the body or out of the body, my request is but request."—
But requests which are made to a power unknown, unseen,
Secret, everywhere present, whose limits are undefinable,
Are really Prayer raised to an inferior god.
And *why* should any man pray to such a being,
Rather than to the highest and purest, the one true God?
Why? but because God's sympathy is doubted,
While the sympathy of the human god is regarded sure.—
When once such a belief is established in the heart,
For one prayer raised to God ten rise to the dæmon,
Who must soon carry off superior affection,
Crushing true religion under baneful idolatry.
Just so did Apollo, Diana, Venus or Hercules,
Mercury or Æsculapius, undermine the worship of Jupiter;
And heroes in turn intercept those other gods' honour.
Just so, in the Christian creed, which professed but One God,
Did Polytheism rise,—yea, and a Queen of heaven,
And angels and spirits of the dead were idolized,
And many a saint with fictitious history.
And many a picture, multiplying one Mary into many.

 To God most high, most just, most holy,
No man dares to raise frivolous petitions or such as he knows to be wrongful;
But a Greek would beseech Artemis to help his murderous raid,
And a Knight Templar implore the Virgin to prosper his adultery.
Prayer is corrupted, thanksgiving is intercepted,
Adoration of the Holiest vanishes from the heart,
When communion with lower gods drives out Divine Religion:
And into this will all Dæmonism gravitate unfailingly.

 Where are the spirits of the departed, we can neither know nor guess.
But, if they exist, all analogy strongly urges
That God lays on them *duties*, (an essential of happiness,)
Whereby their agency is restrained to ends well defined,
With limits of space and of time, as befits finite creatures.
Is it not absurd and childish, to imagine that the finite
Can be at call and listen to our words, as though they were infinite?
Human affection may suggest and defend such fancies;
But thus of old did idolatries arise, and so may they rise again.

NOTE ON VERIFICATION (p. 16).

Fully to discuss Intuition and Verification, would be to write a treatise on the foundations of human knowledge. In my limited reading on such subjects nothing has given me so much satisfaction as Mr. J. Daniel Morrell's four lectures on the Philosophical Tendencies of the Age, (London, 1848,) which closes with the proposition, that "The Final Appeal for the Truth which philosophy embodies, must be to the *universal reason or the common consciousness of mankind.*"

When we can once penetrate to the ultimate principles, which are real foundations, no other Verification is imaginable than agreement with other men and agreement with ourselves. We cannot *argue down* an Insane man nor a pertinacious Criminal: we can do nothing but *overbear them* by our mere numbers and by our internal concord. Neither in physics nor in morals can the laws of proof be proved; they can only be enunciated, and approved: the same is true of primary facts and primary judgments. Whatever atheistic or necessarian logicians may wish or assert to the contrary, there is no more solid foundation for truth than Instinct and Intuition afford when they rest on the collective agreement of mankind; which agreement gives us the very same right to put constraint on an insane man, to punish a criminal, to use invective against a teacher of profligacy, and to dogmatize against an atheist or a necessarian. Up to a certain point, argument is reasonably used; beyond that point it is reasonable to resort to Force against some, to Strong Words against others. If they reject our intuitions, they will naturally regard our facts as "proving nothing;" and immeasurable as is the value of Experience, it has no logical force whatever except by aid of intuitions on which we have to fall back.

Only because it is so hard to reach the really primary intuitions, because those who have little logical culture are apt to mistake their own mingled intuitions, for ultimate human judgments; therefore Verification of every kind is to be diligently sought, and the corrections which it affords are to be prized. Its efficacy in such cases is properly *negative*, to modify or refute supposed intuitions. What it does not destroy, it may often indirectly confirm. But probably the true final result of all such exercise of mind is, to *purify* the power of Intuition itself by removing mists and false lights.

ON THE FUNCTIONS OF UNBELIEF (p. 21).

"To Scepticism we owe that spirit of inquiry, which during the last two centuries has gradually encroached on every possible subject; has reformed every department of practical and speculative knowledge; has weakened the authority of the privileged classes, and thus placed liberty on a surer foundation; has chastised the despotism of princes; has restrained the arrogance of the nobles, and has even diminished the prejudices of the clergy. In a word, it is this which has remedied the three fundamental errors of the olden time: errors, which made the people, in politics too confiding; in science too credulous; in religion too intolerant....

"No single fact has so extensively affected the different nations as the duration, the amount, and above all, the diffusion of their scepticism. In Spain, the church, aided by the Inquisition, has always been strong enough to punish sceptical writers, and prevent, not indeed the existence, but the promulgation of sceptical opinions. By this means the spirit of doubt being quenched, knowledge has for several centuries remained almost stationary. But in England and France, which are the countries where scepticism first openly appeared and where it has been most diffused, the results are altogether different; and the love of inquiry being encouraged, there has arisen that constantly progressive knowledge, to which these two great nations owe their prosperity."—Buckle's '*History of Civilization in England,*' vol. i. pp. 308, 309.

On the importance of the negative and destructive element in the Socratic teaching, see Grote's 'Greece,' vol. viii. ch. 68. pp. 595 608, etc.

SECOND BOOK.

MORAL UTTERANCES.

ABSTRACT TRUTH.

The mind of man is finite, but Nature and Truth are infinite; hence our knowledge is always imperfect: yet by continuous thought knowledge tends perpetually to advance. Continuous thought is not always just thought: yet it is only by continuous thought, handed from mind to mind, and in its course variously tested, that error is cast out, and assurance of truth is earned. The thoughts which we have inherited make us in many things wiser than our fathers; and the better we do our duty, the more likely are our children to become wiser than we. True and healthy Science is ever growing; but unsound Science cannot grow and needs destruction.

The Universe and the Infinite are incomprehensible, but not inscrutable: man's mind is adapted to the study of them. Truth is congenial to man. Moral truth is then most consummate, when, like Beauty, it commends itself without argument. Of the vast Whole we catch but partial and faint glimpses; yet these are to us the dawnings of insight into the Divine.

To revere and to adore some Power above us, from which we spring and on which we depend, is essential to full moral health. Fully to understand that Power is of course impossible; plainly because it is impossible fully to understand ourselves or anything at all. To shape in our minds such an image of the Divine Power, that we may be able to love him, to honour him, to revere, to submit, to put forth aspirations,—is of high value to moral life, and aids morality to assume its spiritual and loftiest form. We cannot comprehend God, any more than a dog can comprehend a man. But as the dog may apprehend his master, so may man apprehend God. God surrounds us; we do not surround him. So far as we are in contact with him we may apprehend him. Moral fellowship is due to our brother-men, while they love goodness as we love it, however they may differ from us in interpreting Divine Power.

FREEDOM FROM ERROR.

Knowledge begins from miscellaneous information, of which much is accurate, and generally some is false. With fresh and fresh additions, what is erroneous is gradually corrected. The errors may have been great or small, but are not necessarily a seed of new error. Copiousness of information being the thing chiefly sought, scrupulous accuracy at first cannot be aimed at.

But in proportion as man becomes a Reasoner, every error is a fertile seed, or one may say a fountain, of new error. Hence in every Science the vital matter is to have no error whatsoever, great or small, in the first principles. To attain a few actual truths, clear from error, is better than ten times as much truth with error mixed; for we want solid foundations to build on. If you build on twelve supports, and one is rotten, that one may cause the whole fabric to fall in. It would have been better to have only six, all firm, and to sacrifice five sound supports in order to get rid of one unsound. So in Science, from one small error mere Reasoning will deduce endless new errors of great magnitude and perhaps of a very pernicious kind. Thus, if in Physiology or in Chemistry or in Anatomy there be some mistake, the reasoner applying it may kill instead of healing a patient. Through some slight error in the principles of Mechanics, and consequently in the rules of shipbuilding, a ship may be constructed which sends a thousand brave men to the bottom of the sea. Entire false Science may arise, as Astrology and Magic, out of such real and noble sciences as Astronomy and Chemistry if a single falsehood take root in the same soil with them. In this sense we may recal the words of a Roman poet, that "the first point of wisdom is to get rid of folly."

These sentences entirely apply to Religion,—even if we may not yet call Religion a science, — because undeniably Religion abounds with Reasoning, and ever aspires to be Science, in proportion as it is sagely cultivated. Often those persons reason most who are unaware that they reason at all; and such reasoners attempt neither correction nor verification. Every error *consecrated* in a religious system has deadly potentiality. Wise men may avoid its poison, but the many seldom escape infection from it.

Consider the awful results of a belief in WITCHCRAFT. Religious men and wise men have been perverted by it into murderers and slanderers on the greatest scale, and have steeled their consciences to horrible cruelties. All the atrocities of so-called Religion, of which the history is heartrending, arose from incorporating some false doctrine with much that was true, so that the true consecrated the false, and the false assumed empire over the soul. In general only exterior science has dispelled the delusion, or exterior force has suppressed it. Religious thought ought to suffice, but it has been paralyzed, because disobedience to some sacred LETTER has been held impious.

Many persons deprecate what they call Destructive or Negative teaching, dreading it as ruinous. But to unteach us an error which has lodged itself on the throne of noble and sacred truth, is nearly the greatest service that any one can do to Religion.

PRAISE AND BLAME.

Human Language no sooner rises above its lowest and most imperfect state, than it contains words made for Praise and Blame. Deeds done under outward constraint, no one blames or praises. They are not regarded as the work of the doer, who is in them a mere tool, reluctant or unconscious. The same holds of deeds done in sleep or in madness or under the power of some drug craftily administered. Men are praised, chiefly when their conduct is better than could reasonably have been expected; they are blamed, chiefly when it was worse than might have reasonably been expected. Whether we praise or blame, we assume their actions to be Free.

Every cultivated language so abounds with words called Moral, as to show that universal mankind believes in human Freedom. The maintainers of Necessity, on the contrary, say, that Freedom is a delusion, and that Man does but fancy himself free, because the constraint is internal, continuous, secret, and without struggle; yet *even they* praise and blame, talk of Virtue and Duty, of what Ought to be, and Ought to have been done. But if only one way is possible, and there is no room for choice, then nothing ought to have been, but what has been. No conduct can then be bad, but as a conflagration is bad: it can no more be vicious or censurable, than a hurricane or an earthquake. It may be good, as the sunrise; but not virtuous or praiseworthy, more than the warmth of the sun or the punctuality of a planet. To praise it or to blame it,—to exhort to greater speed, or to a change of course,—would be absurd. A man's bad deeds would then only be like the devastations of a tiger; there might be a killing, but not murder; ferocity, but not wickedness. Except within the limits of Freedom, there is neither Virtue and Praise, nor Wickedness and Blame.

Besides, it is not true that within the human breast there is *no Struggle*. When temptation assaults one frail in Virtue, the heart is drawn two ways, allured by some desire, yet apprehensive that it is wrong: then often there is perplexity and hesitation, and paralysis of action, until the man himself decides for himself, which of two motives shall be, for him, then and there, the stronger. Until he has made one to be stronger, neither of the two was as yet the stronger. Nor indeed is Effort possible, except to one believing himself free.

By some, who confess that Praise and Blame are inevitable,—who say that man is necessitated to praise and blame, and cannot help it,—it is gravely alleged that EXPERIENCE *justifies* it, by showing that praise and reward are a useful stimulus, blame and punishment a useful deterrent; and that on *this* account they are applied, not because the agent is supposed free. No plea can be more fatuous. *Justification* is superfluous, if the man who praises or punishes cannot help praising or punishing. Lies are as virtuous as truth, cruelty as virtuous as equity, if one cannot help lying and cruelty; that is, there is no virtue and no vice, not so much as in a cow or a pig. These unwise men (men often in many ways estimable) tell us that blame and punishment are a *useful stimulus!* Try how such doctrine (without fraudful reserve) will train up a child. "You have been very naughty, and have told a lie. I am the more ashamed of you, because I know it is in your very nature, and you could not help lying. I do not bid you avoid it, next time you are tempted; for I know you have no choice and are a machine moved by force that is not you: but so am I; and I am going to punish you, because I cannot help it, though I know you do not deserve punishment; but I hope it will do you good," Was ever parent such a fool, as thus to *correct* a child? The alternative is to use fraud, and pretend that the child has freedom, and deserves blame, though the parent, while rebuking the lie of his child, is himself a liar. No one would thus defend the indefensible, except in sticking to a hypothesis.

But again, we are assured that the uniformity of crime, when *averages* of five years are taken, show the crimes to be inevitable.—If there were really, in all times and all places, a strict uniformity of certain actions, it might prove that either Instinct or Habit is so imperious, as temporarily to withdraw that particular class of actions from the catalogue of Freedom and of Morals. Then we should neither praise nor blame them, but submit to them, as we submit to sleep by night: yet no reason would appear for regarding any *other* class of actions to be necessary. But the alleged facts really prove nothing more, than that in a certain city, (say Paris,) there is from year to year no great change in the state of society. There is about the same amount of rascality, of misery, of ignorance, of weakness,—moral and physical; with the same amount of temptation to crime. Pity, rather than indignation, (it may be pleaded) is suitable in such circumstances. To remove or lessen temptation and alter the circumstances, to enlighten ignorance and assist weakness, to address *moral influences* to the brutalized in mind, is eminently needed, more so perhaps than severity, even when severity is indispensable. But to set up the doctrine of Necessity, is *moral despair*, is a proclamation of moral death, is a prohibition to apply regenerating influences.

When a choice of action is claimed as essential to Right and Wrong, no one hereby pretends that Free Will guides all action. Many actions of men, as of all animals, are instinctive or habitual, without moral choice or even moral debate. In proportion as Virtue becomes adult, Freedom ripens and strengthens, which in incipient virtue was weak, or scarcely apparent. Evil habits also enchain the will, so that the votary of vice often is unable to break loose. In all imperfect virtue the power of the Will has its limits, and may be overcome, until Virtue is loved as the chief good. Hence the worldly minded have believed, that every man has his price; only, the virtuous are more cunning and haggle for greater payment! Necessarians who are virtuous in action (as they generally are, though their theory annihilates virtue) are as much concerned as we to spurn such base notions.

Nothing in the Necessarian doctrine is practically worse, than that it explodes self-reproach and contrition for sin, as a folly. King Agamenon in Homer excuses his pride and violence by the plea: "I am not to blame, but Jupiter and Fate and the Fury: what could I do? the god wrought everything. I could not lay aside infatuation, for Jupiter took away my good sense." Thus the Necessarian (if consistent) is self-justifying and self-righteous. But homely wisdom demands contrition of offenders, and never trusts them again, until true contrition appears. Self-reproach after misconduct is essential to the stability and tenderness of virtue, which has no depth of root, nor vigour, nor sweetness, unless the heart is watered by the inward tears of repentance.

Man and the universe are in harmony. It cannot be necessary to man's perfection, that he should believe a lie; but it is necessary to his moral advancement, and to all effort for progress, that he believe his own Freedom. But if Necessarianism were true, Morals and Religion perish at once, and all human language has to be re-made. Freedom of the Will is now impugned chiefly by Materialists or Atheists. Also on the side of Theism Predestinarians have denied it, most of them in so contradictory a way as evidently to refute themselves; for they add, that bad men deserve and receive punishment for their wickedness, hereby conceding that they had a choice to be otherwise: moreover, if even the bad have freedom, much more have the good. But some moderns are aware of this self-contrariety and avoid it; maintaining that Necessarianism reigns universally over *all creatures*, through the high supremacy of the CREATOR, whose will is the sole agent; that there is no merit nor demerit, but only good and evil, better and worse; no room for praise or blame; no room for reward or punishment, but only for spontaneous preference of the better. Such reasoners do not know, that they *first* overthrow all moral ideas as completely as do the materialistic and atheistic Necessarians, (as above set forth) *next*, they destroy all reason for believing in God. For if we know nothing of Will in ourselves, we can have no just ground for inventing the existence of Will and attributing it to an unknown superior being. A God without Will is a blind Fate. We know man first and best; we have but a secondary knowledge of God. If universal mankind testify to the rightfulness of Praise and Blame, of Repentance and Effort, and hereby to a Freedom of Choice, we must not so construct our theory of the Divine Ruler, as to deny this Freedom.

RELIGION.

Heart-worship, not Head-worship, makes a man's religion. Devotion to an Ideal, is worship; the higher the Ideal, the nobler the worship. By devotion to our highest ideal, we expand our minds to embrace what is still higher. By devotion to Self, we quench idealism, and become base.

There is no higher idea of God than Righteousness and Perfection; to follow these is Virtue and Spirituality, and is the only reasonable service of God. Whatever each man worships inwardly, is his God, whether he know it or not. He who has a Ruling Passion, worships one God, good or evil. He who is carried at random by many impulses, has many Gods; perhaps as shifting, as shapeless, as unworthy, as any heathen divinities. He whose ruling passion has Self for its end, is a self-idolator, and worships, not an ideal, but a block, like the stupidest of heathens. There is no real and complete Atheist, but the brute who has no moral choice: that is why common feeling joins Atheism with materialism and brutality.

On the moral choice depends the religion, whether ennobling or debasing. Pure morals and pure religion act and react on each other. Religion is a free service: each chooses his God for himself. If any are votaries of Goodness, they worship God in heart, though they be in head Atheists; and those who in head are Theists are but Pagans and devil-worshippers, when they are votaries of wickedness or folly.

Religion is a powerful passion of the soul, a vehement mover to good or evil. Religious theories have improved and have depraved morals: no mere theory of religion marks the line between good men and bad.

RIGHT AND RIGHTEOUSNESS.

Men learn of Right only through Society; hence, when we speak of Rights, we mean peculiarly mutual and relative rights. The Righteous is he whose heart and life is pervaded by right. Fully to know the right, demands the culture of all our powers.

The righteous not only does right, but loves to do right. The righteous moreover loves that right be done, and has pleasure in those who love to do it: hence he is said to love Righteousness. The righteous reveres righteousness which is loftier than his own, and rejoices at every increase of righteousness everywhere. He does not revere power, when it is disjoined from righteousness. He cannot be envious to see higher righteousness, but he is stimulated by it to imitation.

To love righteousness is a more adult state of goodness, than merely to approve the right. He who loves righteousness hates unrighteousness, and shrinks from unjust men. To approve the right, is the beginning of goodness; to have all the passions right, is the end.

For the full growth of right, *Faith* in Righteousness as the true end of man, is essential. He who is without this Faith, will have no inward power to persevere in right action, when unhappiness follows from it. In heaven or earth is nothing more divine than Righteousness. Wherever is moral life, Righteousness is the highest law.

The true nature of each thing is seen in its highest development. Righteousness is most truly natural to man, precisely because man is made for it, and it establishes his best state, and in it consists his highest development.

VIRTUE.

Righteousness and Virtue and Moral Perfection are but different names for the same idea, coloured by different associations of thought. Man is made for Virtue; if he lives to attain Virtue, he must die rather than forfeit it. Virtue is his Chief Good, and not Pleasure, Ease or other happiness.* This is indeed visible in the fact, that the wise mother desires for her child, rather that he be virtuous, than that he be happy. The virtuous aims at virtue itself as his end, and not at pleasure from virtue.

Freedom to be virtuous is an unalienable right of man. The performance of Indefinite Duties, which Law cannot enforce, is a principal test of

---

* For full discussion and illustration of this cardinal truth, see the noble treatise, entitled, Intuitive Morals, by Frances Power Cobbe.

virtue. There is no Right without Duty, nor Duty without Right. There is no Power without Duty, nor Duty without Power. Every moral nature lives and breathes in Duty.

Prudence is necessary for sustaining man's individuality, and for perseverance in virtue itself. Prudence therefore is a Duty. Prudence performs like services to Virtue, as the Body to the Spirit: yet a character which were nothing but prudent, would not be virtuous. Prudence aims directly to manage the circumstances of the individual: but no circumstantial well-being is Virtue, nor is so valuable as Virtue. Virtue rises out of the force of man's nobler passions, but consists in the rightful harmony of all the impulses.

Moral harmony is the highest element of happiness, which hereby rewards faithfulness to duty; but it is not to be won by the mere outward actions of virtue. The inward actions of the soul are of far more importance to virtue than the outward actions of the body. The actions which we call vicious or wrong do not imply wickedness in a madman: their mischief to others is without, but their wickedness is only in the heart of the doer.

To the Grandeur of virtue, a lofty ideal is requisite, to arouse Aspiration. To keep aspiration within sobriety, and within the possibilities of nature, a wide reach of knowledge is important. Knowledge also stimulates aspiration by example. To forbid Knowledge, is to restrict Wisdom and repress Virtue.

SOCIAL VIRTUE.

Virtue is the perfection of one man, considered in himself; yet without human society virtue could only be in embryo. As no virtue could be perfected in solitude, so can no one man be independent of surrounding virtue or vice. The virtue of each aids the virtue of the rest, nor can any of us be perfected without the rest. The Virtue of each is the Expediency of all.

Degraded classes in a nation taint the moral atmosphere of other classes. Degraded or wicked States and Nations that lie outside of us, will corrupt our national virtue in proportion to the nearness of intercourse. All mankind breathe one air, and each part has a personal interest in the moral health of every other part. All good men are soldiers of virtue, and live for its triumph. The conflict of right and wrong cannot cease; and if the good are negligent, the worse will prevail. By the progress of good, what was once good seems to be bad; because a better than it is revealed. Hence the fight is no sooner won, than it has to be renewed: and so must it be, unless the perfect were attained. But the perfect is unattainable; for it is infinite, and man is finite.

Social evils seem to be deeper and

deeper, the more they are examined. This must not discourage us; for the same thing is found, when we first begin personal examination in earnest: but it calls seriously to a change of course.

Interest and Prudence and Duty alike command all to combine against Social Evils. It is a fanatical religion which forbids such combination. There is no Political action more obligatory on free citizens, than that of insisting that the State shall study primarily the Public Morals. Public Morals cannot be enforced by Liars and Hypocrites. If Statesmen of high virtue cannot be had, yet Statesmen of common Honesty and Truthfulness may be demanded in every Free State. Where Public Falsehood for the convenience of State Policy is regarded as an ordinary duty of Statesmen, the Public Service becomes a moral corruption and a pestilence to the community.

Social Virtue is impossible, unless the daily organs of Social Action co-operate for it. Those organs cannot and will not co-operate, with which it is a received axiom, that Wealth is more important than Virtue. Mammon Worship has its stronghold in Cabinets and Parliaments which disown the function of studying National Virtue. Churches can have no deep nor progressive prosperity, but will gravitate with wealth into worldliness, unless they deliberately take up the practical problem of promoting the National Virtue by purifying the State organs from moral iniquities. Therefore Despotism and Spirituality must for ever be antagonistic.

JUSTICE.

Between man and man or between man and brute, Justice is Righteousness. So also between nations, or between Orders of men, Justice is the law of duty. Justice is, *in the long run*, Expedient for mankind at large, whatever measure of expediency be assumed: but if expediency be judged by any outward or material measure, the Just and the Expedient are by no means identical *in single cases* or in short courses of action. Where Justice has no claims, Expediency is rightly followed; but where each makes a claim, the Just is always to be preferred. Lower animals, as men, have their Rights; and there is a Justice due to them. Through the execrable cruelties of man, the brutes suffer endless torment, which Opinion ought loudly to stigmatize and Law to forbid.

To know rightly what is Just, we must understand the nature of Man and Beast. He who is ignorant, becomes unjust in his deed, even when he is not unjust in his will; and his unjust deeds still engender strife and ill will and violence and depravation. The political wrongs of class to class oftener rise out of negligence and ignorance than out of self-conscious injustice. So do the cruelties of man to brute. As without Knowledge there is no Justice, so without Justice there is no Wisdom.

Justice is righteous and good, whatever shape it take from circumstances. Justice toward the unfortunate is Mercy; Justice toward the guilty is Punishment for the general benefit. If the guilty man after punishment return unreformed into society, he will generally return worse, more dangerous, and in circumstances conducive to new guilt. Unless the guilty are put out of life, there is no safety for the public but in their reformation. An unmoral Power may torture, but cannot punish, any more than reform.

Justice is the cement of mankind. A Nation or Empire which neglects to be internally Just, falls asunder by discord or decay. Love is often a debt of Justice and becomes a happy reality. Universal Kindliness is a debt of Justice.

Without an infinite heart, Universal Love is a delusion. Love which is arbitrarily directed, by one who has heart and means to spare, may sometimes be persevering and fruitful, but will often be disappointing and disappointed. To be first Just, and then Loving, is to advance toward fulness of virtue. To refuse Justice and bestow Love, is an affectation of Mercy and a reality of Insult.

Without Chastity in man, there is no Justice to woman. Political Justice is as essential to moral union, as every other sort of Justice. Women as yet have had no Political Justice.

There is no right Rule, but the Rule of Justice. Obedience to Just Rule is ennobling: all other obedience is prudential only, and is apt to degrade. To strengthen the Unjust, is to injure the Just. Peace without Justice is not Peace, but a Truce of War. Policy which shuts its eyes to Justice, is pernicious folly. Unjust Power is destined for overthrow; the more rapidly, as those over whom it domineers are more virtuous. Without entire Virtue, there is no entireness of Justice; for all Vice disables soul or body for some active service.

THE PASSIONS.

In proportion to the elevation of every creature in the scale of life, the passions are stronger than the appetites. So too are the spiritual passions stronger than the animal passions. Of the spiritual passions, the generous and enthusiastic are adapted to conquer the selfish.

Fanaticism may be defined as ignorant and misapplied Enthusiasm. Fanaticism, equally with Enthusiasm, is a spiritual passion, and may be wholly unselfish: it is therefore apt to be a formidable scourge, by its great energy. Yet to the individual it is less degrading than selfishness. In the long run enthusiasm conquers fanaticism; because fanaticism is undermined by the growth of knowledge, and knowledge tends to increase with time and experience. Hatred is not an ungenerous, but a noble passion, when directed against objects which ought to be hated. He who cannot hate cannot love. Every generous passion aids to purify the whole soul, and adds strength to other generous passions. Every baser passion, when victorious over a nobler, degrades the whole soul, and weakens every nobler passion. Hence the nobler passions are in natural alliance, and so in some sense are the baser. Hence, also, man is apt to gravitate, when he does not aspire.

The intenser the nobler passions, and the wider the knowledge, the greater is the character. No natural impulse is in itself wrong, but every impulse becomes wrong when indulged in preference to one which is higher. The most religious of the impulses, is the passion for moral perfection. In one who believes in God as perfect in Goodness, this passion necessarily takes the form of Reverence for him, culminating into Love. As it is natural and reasonable to love good men, whom we have not seen, yet know and feel to be good, so from the moment that we truly believe in a Good God it is natural to love him. Moreover, it is reasonable that this love should become an overruling passion; not absorbing or starving other right passions, but regulating them all. True religion is Wise and and Spiritual Passion, directed to Goodness, and to Him in whom all Goodness is impersonate.

HAPPINESS.

No two men have the same idea of Happiness, nor has the same man at different times. To talk of the greatest Happiness, is unmeaning, until we know how to compare and measure one sort of Happiness or one constituent of Happiness with another.

Is then mere Contentment Happiness? But the inventor, expounder and glorifier* of the word "Utilitarianism" has avowed that it is "BETTER to be a human being dissatisfied than a pig satisfied; BETTER to be Socrates dissatisfied, than a satisfied fool:" and all but the unwise will agree with him.

To say that Happiness is a "Sum Total of Pleasures" implies all pleasures to be the same in kind and to differ only in degree; which is certainly false. Equally false is it and absurd to treat all Pains as the same in kind, and to be only Negative pleasure, subtractive from the Sum Total. On the contrary, in comparison with some Noble pleasures no number what-

---

* John Stuart Mill.

soever of Ignoble pleasures are collectively deserving of regard; and some Pains are so terrible, that they cannot be annihilated, if even haply they may be allayed, by the presence of the very highest pleasures.

Men aim at definite gratifications of appetite or passion. No man directs his aim at Happiness as a whole; plainly because no image of this whole can be held before the mind to aim at. But if it could, then to make a selfish end the life-long aim would ensure the loss of Happiness.

To seek the content, comfort, happiness of those around us, is amiable; to seek their *Welfare* is wiser and higher. Yet neither is their Welfare measurable by *their* notions of Happiness nor can our conduct be fitly prescribed by *our* sole notions of Happiness; but Justice to them must take precedence of our tastes. Nor can any of us aim at the greatest happiness of *the greatest number*, (a wholly unmeasurable thing)—except by taking Social Virtue as a known rule, and letting happiness take its chance.

To exalt Happiness, as an indefinite Sum of (never mind what) Pleasures that do not entail Pain, into a primary and rightful end to be aimed at; and to assert that the love of Virtue for its own sake is a result of forgetfulness, like the love of gold for its own sake; injuriously degrades Virtue, and, like the Epicurean doctrine of "Pleasure the only Good," will gravitate into a base Materialism, however little the inventor of the theory intended such a result.

UTILITARIANISM.

A thing is called *useful*, when it helps us to get something beyond itself. If this be the only reason for esteeming it, the end which it subserves is higher than itself.

Thus Food, aiding us to Health and Strength, is useful. When Food is taken for mere Pleasure, with no benefit to Health and with some diminution of Strength, it is not even useful, because Health and Strength are higher ends than corporeal pleasure. Much more are they higher ends than Food; for *it* is merely useful, *they* are desired for their own sake.

Health and Strength are subservient to many higher purposes; yet being in themselves desirable, we decline to call them useful, lest we disparage them. So, although a Good Repute for Virtue conduces to getting employment, we cannot style an honourable reputation useful without seeming to degrade it. The Useful is a thing of lower rank: a mere servant to something higher.

Nothing is useful, if there be not things desirable in themselves; a servant implies a master. No arguments from usefulness can decide what things are desirable for their own sake, nor which of two such things is the more desirable, if they be at all of high rank. This also is because the noblest and highest is rather degraded than honoured by considering its utilities. The decision concerning the *rank* of things desirable is made by an inward judgment, by the soul's preference,—upon intuition: and the soundness of the judgment is verified by the convergence of mankind to agreement.

No wise housekeeper, and no wise moralist, has ever despised things useful; but on the mere usefulness of things no moral system can be based.

PLEASURE.

Pleasure is a *result* rising out of the healthy exertion of a natural instinct or faculty. The pleasure degenerates and decays, if it be aimed at directly.

This is extremely visible in the pleasure which accompanies Eating. Also in Bodily Exercise, and in the admiration of beautiful sights and sounds, the direct pursuit of pleasure will be found to produce morbid results. The pleasure from the Insatiable instincts is higher than that from the Satiable; as to the hound the pleasure of hunting than that of eating.

The Generous pleasures are higher than the selfish. High moral pleasure is called Joy: it cannot be selfish. Pleasure from receiving benefits ceases to be selfish, when it calls out Gratitude. The pleasure of Gratitude exceeds the selfish pleasure from the Gift. Love is fruitful of Joy, blessing alike giver and receiver. When Duty and Honour call for it, there is doubtless a stern joy in sacrificing life.

The pleasures of Knowledge excel in permanence. They become unselfish, and multiply themselves, by calling out the desire to Impart knowledge. Pleasure from the admiration of Beauty or Melody refines, but is peculiarly liable to enervate, from the difficulty of discriminating between following the Instinct and following the Pleasure. To seek for the Pleasure or the Joy as the end of the action, whether in Munificence, in Gratitude, in religious Worship, in the pursuit of Knowledge, in Self-Sacrifice, ruins the virtue as well the pleasure. Pleasure comes not at call; but (under healthy conditions) to those who call her not, she comes often.

A man may be devoted to elegant Art, and remain earnest in his heart, and be ennobled by it; but if he is devoted to the *pleasure* of Art, he becomes enfeebled. Every votary of pleasure, however high in kind, is selfish, and misses the best enjoyment. Hence the most refined Epicurean is apt to lose all relish of pleasure and to tire of life. The votary of many elegant pleasures is justly called Dissipated. When Art or Scenery is loved for itself, its lover desires others to see and love it; thus also the love becomes unselfish, and the pleasure also is heightened.

In so far as enjoyment must be selfish, it is heightened by the smallness of effort and of mental study for the pleasure. While to hold up *any* pleasure as the end of action is a mistake or a mischief, to devote effort and study for animal and satiable pleasure as the end is fitly styled Impure. It makes the Spirit a minister to the Flesh. The brute cannot be impure, since he has no Reason nor Imagination to prostitute. The morbidly Ascetic erroneously treats animal pleasure as in itself (more or less) impure, and tries to reduce it to its lowest point. But animal pleasure is as pure as all other pleasures, provided that it do not occupy premeditation, but comes spontaneously in an act otherwise moral, as *all* pleasure ought to come.

The mischief of sensuality to the whole character depends on the proportion of energy spent in contemplating and contriving for pleasure. An energetic nature may suffer comparatively little harm from such impurity as occupies but a small portion of life and effort. Nevertheless, if it seem to affect the moral character but little, yet it is deadly to the spiritual. Spiritual religion is a severe test to impurity and to sentimentalism, just as to self-admiration. When the soul has defiled itself by the study of pleasure, it finds its access to a holy God blocked up. Hence the aversion of spiritual men to what is called Gaiety; that is, to the elaborate pursuit of elegant Pleasure.

By *Sentimentalism* is meant the seeking for some moral *Pleasure* as an end of action. This also is vicious, enfeebling, debasing; and ruins its own effort.

CONJUGAL RELATIONS.

Instinct, whether in man or in brute, by its very nature is blind, and subserves ends uncontemplated by itself, yet evidently designed by another. Hence the old saying, God is the soul of the brutes. So too the instinct which guides Man to Woman subserves high purposes beyond its own prevision. As generous minds admire most the qualities in which they are deficient, so each sex admires in the other the excellencies most opposite to its own. Respect and admiration, sufficient to lead to the desire of *permanent companionship*, are the proper foundation of conjugal love. Vows of permanent union are no artificial bondage to true lovers: on the contrary, an unwillingness to enter into them would imply the absence of true love. The desire of temporary union is but basely called Love; for it does not seek the welfare of her whom it courts. Rather, (to borrow nearly the words of an old Greek,) As wolves love lamb, so do rakes love their mistresses. Conjugal love cannot exist, without arousing a desire of tender intimacy; from which accrues a Pleasure, proportioned to the intensity of Love. Yet to make such Pleasure a direct object of contemplation and pursuit, tends to destroy it; and is a debasement to the marriage-union, a real impurity. If the married fall into such error, it is at least hidden from foreign eyes, it does not contaminate others, and probably very soon corrects itself. But any union of man and woman which is avowedly temporary, proclaims itself to be impure, is a social contamination, and tends to propagate its own evil. Nor can it be replied, that the temporary union seeks not for Pleasure, but seeks for Progeny. For Progeny needs the tender care of both parents, and is the strongest of all reasons for their permanent union. Persons who live in impure relations are justly shunned in society, so far as other duty may permit; because their example is contaminating.

Marriage is not a device for allowing lower passions to be unbridled; scarcely would a wild polygamy effect this: but it is a state eminently conducing to purify the passions and lead to their rightful control. To esteem Marriage a mere contract between two persons, is a cardinal and most pernicious mistake, The contract between the two must be witnessed by a third, whose presence makes the Community a third party in the covenant. The priest, chancellor or registrar, is the proxy of the Community; which dictates to him on what terms he shall pledge its assent and co-operation. Men and women whose heart is right, are faithful in marriage and observant of duty to children, even when they erroneously think that the Community has no right to concern itself in their union. Their conduct follows their heart, and they are good, though their theory is bad. Such persons very rarely affront the public by disdaining legal marriage. There is no more pernicious theory than that of Free Love, with its inevitable results of infanticide and abortion, or of children cast as orphans on the community. This is a training to wickedness. If in any State the law of marriage be unjust, those who rebel against it must do as did the Quakers, —summon kinsfolk and friends as witnesses to marriage, avoiding everything clandestine.

Marriage vows, being mutual, presuppose mutual faithfulness, and in no case can prejudge the question of Divorce necessitated by unfaithfulness. Cruelty, in its many forms, is the worst kind of unfaithfulness. Divorces by an impartial court, with degradation to the offending party, do not lower the sanctity of marriage. To sustain conjugal rights when they have been flagrantly forfeited, is a dishonour to marriage. Divorce which affects to replace both parties unblemished into the unmarried state, cannot be easy and speedy of attainment, without extreme danger to public morals. Nevertheless, if several years of legal *Suspension* intervene, ultimate Divorce is not necessarily a public evil. *Absolutely* to refuse Divorces to women who married under parental pressure, is a real and great injustice. As Nuns ought to be allowed to repent of their vows, so ought the married, under such limitations *only* as the public morality vehemently demands. Courts formed chiefly of kinsfolk and near friends, conducting their inquiries privately, are the most obvious umpires of such questions; and if the reasons of their verdict are made public, no evil seems to arise from the privacy.

Marriage is a deep moral interest to all, and to many a great spiritual aid; but to call it in any other sense a *necessity* to ordinary men, is against the plainest facts. Such a belief, (inculcated sometimes by the profligate, oftener by erring religion,) is most pernicious to young men, and totally misdirects the mind. Far worse is the profligate audacity of a medical school, puffed up by State-patronage, and by a belief that it is scientific. Its members having largely been corrupt from early youth, teach young men that fornication under clever medical management is the only way of health. Governments which become their docile pupils and tyrannical tools, will be involved in common overthrow with foul and fatuous teachers.

A deplorable mischief encountered by many men (which more than anything else involves "civilized" society in horrors)—is the defilement of the imagination during boyhood. Nothing so effectually washes this away, as a virtuous and reverential love.

Woman is made for the purification and softening of Man: Man for the strengthening of Woman.

CHURCH AND STATE.

No existing Government wholly fulfils the idea of a State, nor any existing Theocracy the idea of a Church. State and Church are *Ideals*, to which we approximate. The State must not be a brute force of compulsion, nor the Church an arbitrary power of dictation: though the one wield power and the other put forth doctrines: but each is responsible to reason. The perfect State is conformed to Justice, the perfect Church to Truth. Yet the State is compulsive, and the Church is voluntary. For the State commands action, and the Church studies wisdom. The State is the organization of a people's chief strength, and is co-extensive with the idea of the nation. The Church organizes moral wisdom, and may either overlap and embrace many nations, or comprize only a part of one nation. Thus there may be many Churches in one people, or many peoples in one Church; but there can only be one State to one people.

Morality is the common concern of State and Church; but the State dictates that morality only which can be enforced, namely, that which can be defined in the words of law: such are external, mutual, and definite duties. Nevertheless, the State can immensely benefit moral practice indirectly; first, by making every fundamental institution just; next, by such enactments as tend to set the habits of every class towards industry, sociability, and outward virtue. The Church rises above these, and exhorts man's conscience to indefinite duties and to inward sentiments. Thus the State enacts laws concerning conduct and rights, the Church utters principles concerning truth and righteousness.

When the chief strength of a nation is no longer in the organs of State, revolution is nigh at hand; when the chief wisdom of a nation is unorganized, the real Church is nonexistent. There is no higher interest of each citizen than to have virtuous fellow-citizens; hence there is no more direct function of the State than to promote the public virtue. It were monstrous if the State could only fine, whip and hang, and might not prevent from crime. Virtue of course must be interpreted from no sectarian standard; but from broad experience and the general consent of human law. To suppress Public and Contagious Immorality is among the most urgent duties of the State; to preach against it, is a primary duty of the Church. Immorality becomes most Contagious, when it is the basis of a Traffic, and draws capital into it as an investment. Traffic in Immorality is a conspiracy against the most vital interests of the community.

No immorality is more fruitful of manifold mischief to the community, than the seduction of young women: none is more fatal to spiritual interest. There is no wickedness against which Church and State are more solemnly bound to combine, than this. There is no wickedness which more detestably disgraces Christendom, in Church and State alike.

Apathy and neglect of Church and State towards palpable and undefended moral enormities is the worst mark of deep-seated corruption. Corruptions not perceived, and left to be inveterate, engender inward decay, and finally revolution, hitherto generally violent.

THE CHURCH INTERNALLY.

The Church (in its essence) is not a Congregation, though parts of it congregate: Nor is it a confederacy for some one practical end, though it serve many practical ends: Nor does it aim to supersede free inquiry, though it proclaim attained truth: Nor does it enter party-politics, though it give a new soul to policy: But the Church is essentially a union of persons professing a common faith concerning moral and spiritual things, and aiming to extend the belief and practice of that faith. In proportion to the depth and grandeur of the truth professed, and the intensity of faith, is the efficiency of the Church for good.

Where faith is clear and strong, its voice is mostly heard in Prophecy. Prophecy* is not rightly understood to mean prediction of the future, except so far as moral wisdom knows the issues of right and wrong. The Prophet in ancient times spoke rebuke and exhortation, edification or comfort: his predictions were secondary, and not always true. All past time witnesses that false prophecy was mixed with true, and that a discrimination between them was needed. Prophecy therefore does not supersede, but stimulates, free thought and judgment in the hearer. The Church ought to be its collector, its judge, its sifter, and the editor of all that is best. Thus the Church may organize Prophecy, though she cannot create it.

The treatment of Enthusiasts by the Church of Rome indicates some apprehension of this function in the Church. The ambition of the same Church to dictate the measures of public policy was but an exaggeration and extravagance of a sound moral instinct. For, it must always be a just aim of every true Church to impress a pure moral purpose and moral sentiment on the State and on public men.

As in the halls of Judgment, so in the Chambers and Cabinets of Statesmen, many questions are debated which mere Religion cannot solve, and in which the Church must not interfere: yet, that Judges and Statesmen should sincerely make the Right and the Just their first object, is a topic on which the Church may cry aloud. Through the ambition of civil governments to control religious freedom, the moral functions of the State have been perniciously denied and forgotten. Through the ambition of priesthoods to cripple social and political freedom, the political duties of Religion are perniciously overlooked or mistaken.

SACRED BOOKS.

Out of the multitude of hymns and prophecies poured forth by Hebrew bards, the judgment of Hebrew piety picked and kept many which have since been honoured as inspired by God. So out of the many narratives of the life of Jesus, the Christian Church selected *four* for peculiar reverence; not because they were known to be historically true, but because they were felt to be morally profitable. We may not blame them for this: for of historical

---

* Prophecy is a Greek word and means *Forth-Utterance.* So the Latin *Profari.*

truth a Church is a very bad judge, but of moral excellence a good Church judges wisely. So again out of many letters written by Christian teachers, the Church adopted some as pre-eminently good; and after the sifting of two centuries fixed a canon of the New Testament.

Books thus pre-eminently honoured by the voluntary selection of piety, are reasonably held to be Sacred, in a high and peculiar sense; and such books may fulfil a high function in moral history, as have the sacred books of India, Persia, Judæa and Christendom. Their benefit nevertheless has been grievously lessened by the strong tendency of mankind to idolize and lift into ideal perfection whatever has engaged their sacred feelings. Hebrew and Christian books for which the writers advanced no high pretensions have thus been gratuitously and hurtfully exalted into a miraculous greatness. Even the Confessions of Faith put forth by Protestant Reformers have been in most countries pushed into unnatural and absurd eminence. Such a process generally imposes upon others the disagreeable duty of appearing as depreciators of books once valuable.

When Books and Men are treated with sober honour, we may revere them not soberly only, but sometimes passionately: but where they have been made objects of idolatry, the same thing is dangerous both to ourselves and to others. It is then seldom possible for the many to regain a just estimate of them, without an interval of neglect. Hymn Books have been to the Protestant Churches the chief representative of new sacred writings. No Bibliolatry has been paid to them, and none have more effectually promoted spiritual life. All Sacred Books, however valuable, must be pervaded by the errors of their age, and unless variously purged and modified, become unfit for practical use to generations which have unlearned those errors.

TEACHING AND PUBLIC PRAYER.

Self-taught men see vividly what they see, and are often deep, if narrow; but one mind unaided must learn to great disadvantage. The larger the accumulations of knowledge the more do we need teaching, and chiefly the teaching of books. Wise teaching saves the learner from many wanderings and from waste of effort. The wise teacher knows when to argue, and when to dictate; and the wise learner will submit to each in its turn. When the teacher proposes an argument, it is the duty of the learner to canvass the argument and cast aside the authority of the teacher. When the teacher announces a truth to be received on his authority, the learner must receive it *as such*, and expect hereafter to know it more fully.

Knowledge is not complete, while anything remains which is believed on the authority of an individual: nor has the teacher finally done his work, until he has made his authority needless. Young people must believe many things on the authority of elders: because neither the faculties nor the experience of the young are ripe for judging. all things: but authority is a temporary expedient, to save the learner from buying knowledge or wisdom too dearly.

Practical Arts are taught by example joined with precept. Prayer, which is a practical Exercise, is also taught by example. Every printed book of Prayer, or of Psalms and Hymns, is a teaching to pray and to praise God. It stimulates the reader by example; but he has not learnt his lesson, until he prays without the book, not in its words, but from his own heart. As no two hearts are the same, nor have the same wants, so neither can the most special prayers of two hearts be exactly alike. As no two have had exactly the same history, nor enjoyed the very same series of blessings, nor felt the same joys with the same vividness, thanksgiving naturally varies from heart to heart. The prayer and the thanksgiving which is most special from each man is deepest from each man. Hence the private exercises of the heart are naturally deeper than the public.

Public Prayer and Praise may be (in an ideal state of goodness) the natural and impulsive outpouring of a common feeling; and as such, eminently suitable to a high state of religion. When it is not this, it is ordinarily less congenial to a strongly religious mind than similar Private exercises. But to beginners in religion it may be of high value, as a teaching to pray by example. Yet alas! it may also be a teaching of hypocrisy. To teach to children prayers unfitted for children, cannot fail to teach hypocrisy, if it teach them anything. To most persons, in our existing imperfection, the chief use of Public prayers is to teach Private prayer: and the efficacy of the public institution may be roughly measured by the degree to which it excites and maintains private devotions, suggested by the heart itself, in its own words.

REBUKE AND PROPHECY.

Some truths are believed by all the wise and good, yet for that very reason are seldom uttered among equals: they are always taken for granted. In the last four hundred years of active thought and accumulating knowledge, the number of such truths has greatly multiplied. To gather and enunciate such truths is not superfluous, when they are despised by the reckless. Far older truth is every day despised. The highly educated like to assume, but like not to enunciate, moral maxims; yet for the instruction of learners it is not useless. All well proved maxims, when uttered, may be uttered magisterially, and they are peculiarly adapted for Rebuke.

Rebuke, to do good, must generally be impersonal: most men are too proud to endure personal rebuke, when they have deserved it. Not even a friend can often rebuke with good effect; much less could any official teacher rebuke those unknown to him. If a general maxim, uttered in public, is felt by one person as a rebuke, it is because his conscience tells him that he deserves it: thereby he rebukes his own self. Such rebukes are highly profitable. This also is a main function of Prophecy, to rebuke every form of sin and moral evil, without personal assumption.

Prophecy is altogether impersonal. Ask not who is the prophet, nor where. Claim no copyright for his words: truth is not his, but yours, yet not yours only: it is common. All moral wisdom is common property. The prophet has received truth freely, and imparts it freely. Prophecy has a form of its own, which is not accidental. It does not argue, but dogmatizes; it is therefore short and imperative. Bad men will not attend to long sermons, be they ever so well reasoned; and it is easy to forget them: but ten words of denunciation which the guilty man knows to belong to him, may be as an arrow in his side.

Prophecy against evil rouses also the conscience of the many to put away the evil, if they have been blameable in overlooking it. True prophecy deals not in enigmas nor in fanciful conceits; even if sometimes prudentially it have hidden itself in allegory. Nor does it descend to individual cases, in which none may dogmatize, except a judge commenting on a verdict. But though warlike, it shuns to be pugnacious; and though enthusiastic, is eminently practical. Prophecy best undermines religious error, without specific controversy, by calm enunciation of truth. All truth is a rebuke to error; and truth which does not win upon error cannot itself be pure. The purehearted and sound-minded are the fit judges of Prophecy: as also they are the fit rulers of the Church.

EDUCATION.

Education consists in training the Faculties to full self-possession, the Habits to industry and refinement, the Sentiments to rightfulness and warmth. We may passively receive a stock of knowledge, without having the faculties active and well subordinated. Mere Knowledge does not suffice for Wisdom, which depends on a well-balanced Judgment and right Sentiment. Nor ought men to be called Educated, when they have merely learned to obey; but much rather when they have attained Self-guidance. To use Power aright, is a great test of sound education. The uneducated either uses it badly, or, as if terrified by its possession, drops it from his grasp.

Leisure is a great power; and to use Leisure aright, is also a mark of the educated. Without some Leisure, none but a narrow and accidental cultivation of the mind is possible. The millions of England have one-seventh part of time as Leisure: but they do not employ this for any real or valuable education, chiefly because they are not educated enough to estimate the advantage; partly also, because those who ought to assist it, impede it.

Where no literature exists, the illiterate are not necessarily uncultivated; for, the culture of the people diffuses itself in other channels. But where literature is highly developed, unacquaintance with letters generally marks total neglect of cultivation. Differences of wealth and of knowledge do not hinder friendship: but between the refined and the unrefined friendship is impossible. Some, otherwise uneducated, become highly refined in feeling, through the influence of religion alone. Brahmins and Turks have grace and dignity through religion and from general respect. All classes of England would become more refined, if the educated respected them more.

Where trades are apt to be ruined and superseded from public causes beyond the control of the labourer, public justice as well as expediency demands that the State busy itself to secure versatile powers of industry in the working classes. The Primary education of the multitude has two principal roots, Industrial Art and Poetical Recitation. Industrial Art furnishes the labourer with the power of physical support, and in its higher forms rises into Science. Poetical Recitation teaches Moral Sentiment, Musical Rhythm, Refinement, Imaginative Beauty, pride in Nationality, Patriotism. It culminates into Religion.

In the present condition of Trade and complex Constitutions, some instruction in Political Economy and Politics is essential to national well-being: but at what age and through what organs it will best be communicated, remains a question. Religious Institutions might be and ought to be the most efficient educators of the Sentiments; but unhappily, a great change must pass on existing Churches before they can regain the lead which they have lost. Atheism would starve sentiment, Pantheism would corrupt morals. Sectarianism hinders all national religion and sound national education. Theism is the only cure. When it has once fair play, it will educate nations and unite the world in harmony as yet unimagined.

SHORT CREEDS.

The Mussulman has a short creed: "There is no god but God, and Mohammed is his Prophet." Speak to a Mussulman on religion, and he will never reply: "I have no time for such deep inquiries; I am too busy a man of the world." The Christian often so replies, because his creed is complex and of indefinite extent. The short creed spreads over all society, leaving very few unbelievers or scorners. The long creed makes the majority abandon religion to a clergy. If the short creed generates a superficial religion, it is because the creed is intrinsically superficial. The long creed, by the enormous study which it claims and obtains of a few, results in in a religion far deeper than that of the Mussulman. The long creed, by the endless controversies and animosities which it entails between good men, gives to the lazy and the worldly a plausible excuse for neglecting religion. It is no mere pretence, but a terrible reality, that when a plain and busy man wants religion for practice, he finds himself entangled in unmanageable intellectual controversies. "Religion is just what everybody differs about: why should I teaze myself with it?" is the saying of many well-meaning men. Yet it is certain that there are essential foundations of religion in which Christians, Jews and Mussulmans agree; and these suffice for all the exigencies of life. The agreement of all the foremost races of mankind, yields the following short creed: "God is a righteous Governor, who loves the righteous and answers prayers for righteousness."

THIRD BOOK.

RELIGIOUS LIFE.

CALL TO GOD'S SERVICE.

Consecrate yourselves to God, all ye youths and maidens!
Ere the world benumb your fresh feeling or sin harden your conscience.
Know that others have found God, as ye have not yet found him;
But seek ye after him, and ye shall find him also:
Delight yourselves in him, and he shall give you the desire of your hearts.
Seek him in the open field or in the shrouded wood,
Under the evening sky or in the solitary chamber.
Take with you words, and turn to him, and say:
"Oh Author of our spirits, Perfecter of souls,
With thee strength dwelleth in repose, and no passions are in discord;
But the passions of youth are untamed, and we do but move toward perfection,
And Desire often seduces from Goodness, or Ease deters from Duty.
Yet wisely were we made by thee, and thy Will must be best for us;
Early to submit were our prudence, and sweetly to obey, our happiness;
And when we know that we seek thy will, we know that we become thy servants.
Lo! here we resign all baser desire, we consecrate ourselves to be thine.
We will struggle to be as thou approvest; to be pure, as thou art pure,
Unwarped by perverse passion, unspoiled by selfishness,
Active for every good work, sympathizing with every good cause,
Haters and scorners of the wrong, lovers of good and of good men.
So will we aspire to thee, that we may be thine now and alway,
To live before thy open eye, and to die into thy secret bosom."
Speak to him thus, or to this effect, knowing that he reads all your heart;
Knowing that his light searches your dark corners, and sees your unknown faults.
Fear not to meet his piercing gaze, shrink not from his eyes of flame,
But stand before them true-heartedly, to let them burn up your sin.
Oh, how will it cleanse your conscience and strengthen your best purposes!
How will it put to shame all unkindness, all impurity, all worldliness and pride!

Ye who admire heroism shall grow heroic, and the compassionate more tender,
And the generous more self-sacrificing, and the prudent more self-possessed.
Every virtue shall be strengthened, and every vice shall be crippled,
From the day that ye solemnly consecrate your all to the Ever Present God.
For every impulse shall fall into its own place, and learn its due subordination,
And become the meek minister of the soul, or the pleasant amuser of its weariness,
The strong combatant for the right, or the sharp hunter after the true.
And your natures shall become enlarged, as they expand toward God:
Your insight shall be deeper and your survey broader,
Your selfishness shall become prudence, and your prudence unselfish,
Loving your neighbours, loving your country, and mankind, and the Right.
When the faithless trembles at truth, your faith shall but grow stronger,
And where the hypocrite is feeble, your sound heart shall be mighty.
Only aspire after perfection, and tell this out to God,
And ere long ye shall find him and know his exceeding great joy.
He shall fill you of his own fulness and visit you with his Spirit,
And he shall be your trusted Lord, and ye shall be his conscious servants,
Equipped for life and careless of death, aspiring after eternity,
Sighing over your own unworthiness, yet certain of Almighty Love.

POSTURES OF DEVOTION.

Between the body and the mind of man is a close sympathy,
But the mind is the natural ruler, the body is the servant,
Obeying and denoting the inward actions.
The postures of reverence, of desire, of hope are not arbitrary:
They are prompted by nature, and their absence would be unnatural.
So too when a man addresses God, if the heart be chastened,
The voice, the countenance, the whole body will duly sympathize;
And if solitude be granted, and no circumstances hinder,
Most natural is it for the worshipper to abase himself before God,
Whether by sinking on the knee or by momentary prostration,
Or by lowly sitting on the ground with face upturned;
Or otherwise by reverential standing with hands uplifted.
He who waits meekly on his lord with collected mind,
Cannot use frivolous motions or careless demeanour:
And though wisdom forbids any painful postures,
Or whatever by its annoyance may distract from devotion,
Yet equally does it dissuade such luxury of ease

As may tend to slumber and to the lulling of the mind.
Strong and weak bodies have their several properties,
Nor may one herein become a law to another.
Yet each who is upright, and seeks after God,
Learns easily in what postures he is most collected,
Least prone to wanderings or diversion of thought.
Those postures are to *that* man rightful and religious.
Let not one presume to dictate absolutely to another,
Yet let none treat these matters as small or unimportant.

There is a scrupulosity, which makes some men unhappy,
If from morning to evening they have not sunk upon the knee ;
As though kneeling were prayer, or were essential to worship.
This is a weakness, and may be called a superstition :
Yet *if* a man have not yet learned to worship otherwise,
To *him* the loss is grave, when life's hurry forbids to kneel ;
And if he persevere in conscientiousness, his weakness will drop off.
More pernicious is the error of that overbold spirituality,
Which, trusting to its inward power, disuses formalities altogether.
For though, in the flood-tide of some holy sentiment,
When God's glorious mercy has thrilled through veins and heart,
Worship and aspiration, whether one stand, walk or sit,
May seem natural as breath, in every free interval ;
Yet none may expect such heavenly frames to abide
Without his own fostering and without thoughtful effort.
Nay, the more we are favoured by the instirrings of God's Spirit,
The more anxiously must we cherish and invite that presence
By sacred meditation and by solemn seeking ;
Lest we lose spiritual life, by trusting to that which is attained.

By all means then, if possible, *live* in worship and in aspiration ;
But in order that it may be possible, arouse yourself to effort,
Waiting on and seeking after the Unseen at set time and place ;
Addressing him by formal act and in solemn postures,
Not perhaps for many minutes, yet surely with collected earnestness ;
Nor subjecting your liberty to other men's command ;
Yet wisely using the experience of others,
Until it be superseded by fuller experience of your own.
So shall forms help life, and become full of life,
And nature shall grow spiritual, and God's spirit be our nature.

JOY AND CONSOLATION.

Joy is not to be expected from meditations on an Afterworld,
On which some would have our minds fondly dwell.
For by the wisdom of our God no material is surely given,
On which either desire or imagination may repose.
Otherwise, might preoccupation of heart on a nobler scene
Draw away energies needed for improving the present.
A little garden in this world is given for our culture,
Little in itself, great for us, too great alas! for most of us.
On this must we bestow ourselves, undistracted by the future;
Just as the sailor in a strong breeze, when sails are to be shifted,
Thinks not of his country nor of his wife nor even of his God,
But of the sails and of the ship, of the winds and waves.
Yet the knowledge that he has a country and a home recruits his forces,
Filling his heart at short intervals with pleasant memories,
And stimulating him in turn with sweeter hopes.
So may the belief in a future, hidden deep in the background,
Be as a fortress of support to spirits that else might faint,
When the armies of Evil are mighty, and God seems not to rule.
  In truth Joy must not be sought for, or it never will be won;
But Consolation may justly be sought by the heart outworn,
And Consolation is a precious balm sometimes possible to be given,
In calamity, under oppression, and under loss by death.
Hopes of a future life afford topics of comfort,
Only where speaker and hearer have a common faith,
And this is in truth far rarer than some imagine.
Where faith or care of a future life is weak,
Scarcely will you comfort a mourner by asserting it.
Or if a man mourns lawfully, yet selfishly,
For having lost one who was useful and a present comfort,
One who was not loved with pure unselfish love,
Poor is the consolation to the mourner, that his lost friend lives.
He grieves for his own present loss, which is real and solid,
Unchanged and unchangeable by spiritual doctrine.
Worldly sorrows crave worldly reliefs,
Except where the crisis may lift the heart above itself.
Yet the father will not regain his child, nor the wife her husband;
And as to the positive loss, so far as it is personal,
If religion supply it, this is by the doctrine of a Present God,
Sympathizing, supporting, ordaining wisely,

Not by the doctrine of a Hereafter, which still withholds the lost.
Never will faith be strengthened by exercise too hard.
Spiritually to believe in a Heaven, is an act for the spiritual;
To rejoice that a lost friend is there, belongs to the unselfish.
To the many, a better consolation is sympathy and small kindness,
And pointing to like sorrows which have been bravely borne,
And to the duties which forbid too absorbing a regret.
Such topics Nature everywhere teaches to the tender,
And the tender heart which uses them is itself a consolation,
Tho' wrapt in dark Paganism or in lonely Atheism.
But blessed are those who find God's Love ever present,
Light amid darkness, peace amid confusion,
A true Consolation, a solid present fact.
Such men and women exist, under more than one creed.
If faith cannot alway be joyful, yet may it alway be strong,
Comforted by the fixed assurance, that God *even now* reigneth.

DESPONDENCY OF PROVIDENCE.

Who art thou, O man, that mournest inwardly, and sayest:
"I cannot rejoice in God, although I revere him.
I long to believe in his Judgments and to know his Providence;
But my hope is faint and feeble, and will not rise into Faith,
When I see the prevalence of wickedness; and alas! I am sad of heart;
For it seemeth that those who most love God and most ought to live,
May perish earliest and for ever, by reason of their love to him.
Therefore I am downcast, and I cannot rejoice in God,
If it is to signify nothing before long, of what kind men are."
Such thoughts are burthening indeed, and cannot be scolded away:
For even if they be faithless, yet faith comes not by self-reproach.
Yet of *one* thing ought every one to be sure, that *all God's ways are right;*
And if we knew them more fully, the wise would justify all:
Nor can that sadness be right, which surmises that he is wrong;
But as God rejoices in his work, so shall we, when wise, rejoice in it.
If therefore he has caused thee to revere him, and has won thy heart,
See how reasonable and rightful it is to be cheerful and courageous.
If sin have seduced thee, be sad on thy own account; but be not sad for his doings:
Yea, tho' this be thy last hour, rejoice in God's greatness;
Rejoice to believe that the All mighty is All wise and All good:

Rejoice that thou art admitted to bow before him.
Rejoice that thy past and thy present do not darken his face,
But thou mayest gaze straight into its blessed mysteriousness.
What art thou, to be honoured by a consciousness of his presence?
What is his condescension, to dwell within thee and guide thee!
Look not to the dark outside of other men's fortunes;
(For, God's purposes ill show on the surface to the half-wise;)
But look into thine own heart, whereon he has written his law,
And if thou art just and kind, be sure he is juster and kinder.
He doeth, and will do, all things aright, now and hereafter,
All things for thee, all things for all; for none is like to him.
He is alone in his immensity and in his majestic loveliness,
Which sheds calm peace on the heart which seeks his loneliness.
Trouble not thyself to search into his government of the world,
Until first thou hast learned to rejoice absolutely in him.
Rejoice in his goodness, I say, rejoice in his wisdom;
For to believe his goodness and wisdom is a mere rudiment of Faith.
After thou art become full of peace from Faith, with some faint joy,
Then Insight may increase, and new Faith from Insight:
And *afterward* mayest thou discern spiritual things spiritually,
And more profitably search into God's government of the world,
When gladdened by simpler trust and made wise by livelier hope.
For despondency is a bad counsellor concerning the works and ways of God,
And the faithless, who wants to see all, dooms himself to know nothing.

MODERN MARTYRDOM.

In things spiritual, as in mechanism, the strain should fall upon the strong,
Who ofttime suffers for the weaker, yea and by the weaker;
Nor does the wisest man easily become known to the many.

For if a man a little surpass his fellows in wisdom,
And largely share their errors, they can estimate his wisdom,
And knowing him superior, they may even gladly submit,
And choose him to be their leader, their teacher or their magistrate.
Men thus superior are valuable in daily life,
Needful, and never to be despised, but surely worthy of honour.
Yet from such men new principles do not easily come forth;
Rather, their task is to bring out the best from old principles,
And save what is old and good, but to discourage the new.

Also, sharing the errors of the crowd, they love its sympathy,
And fear to lose reputation, if they gain new light too fast.
   For if a man largely surpass his fellows in wisdom
And forsake many of their errors, they ill discern that he is wise;
For, the unwise have no test of wisdom, when it is far above them.
If he have knowledge which they appreciate, or station and birth,
He may thus win respect, and lessen evil suspicion.
But if his wisdom be only moral, spiritual, religious,
Yet subversive of ideas which time has consecrated,
The more surpassing is his wisdom, the greater is the public odium.
For, time is naturally regarded as the test of truth,
And to oppose what all believe seems to be a proof of falsehood,
Nay, and seems to uproot all foundations of belief:
For, the unthinking forget that their nation is not the world,
And the many know not what other nations believe,
Nor what meed of honour is due to foreign thought.
Hence evil surmise, slander, ill-will and hatred
Fall naturally to the lot of those eccentric in religion,
Whether in truth they are much above or much below the nation.
   Such suspicions are inevitable; nor need they be deadly,
But will have healthy action when we are a little wiser,
When humility and justice take deeper root.
For, no principles of man's nature which are of deep necessity
Can ever be wholly bad, or without appointed duty;
So too what is called Bigotry has its rightful place,
Though, when duly corrected, we cease to call it Bigotry.
For lightly to propound novelties is an evil work,
And lightly to unsettle men's notions on things sacred
Is a grave social offence, much to be reprobated.
And if, through mere ignorance unavoidable to man,
A wise innovator is awhile looked on as a mountebank,
And meets with suspicion, aspersion and various losses,—
Loss of friends, loss of promotion, of trade and money,—
These are the payment which he makes in proof of earnestness,
A payment guaranteeing that he shall say nothing lightly,
And distinguishing him from those who trade in novelty.
Nor do these losses permanently repress truth,
For they leave to him life, the means of life, and free speech;
And if truth is a little retarded, yet it takes deeper root.
Such are the worst mischiefs which Bigotry brings,
Where Justice is strongly upheld by impartial law:

And they will yet be further lessened, when justice occupies the heart,
And kindliness is allowed sway, and calm thought is stronger.
    Under dark Superstition, when it holds the scourge of Law,
Deadly indeed are the horrors worked by Bigotry;
Especially where dynastic and priestly jealousy are combined.
Awful have been the sufferings of the martyrs* of truth,
Great still are their hardships in many places.
So much the more must those, who are in comparison free,
Bear lightly that which remains for Conscience' sake,
Aware that if all shrink to suffer at all for truth,
Truth can never obtain advocacy or proclamation.
    Alas! can those be zealous for truth at all,
Or conscious of higher knowledge, or faithful to their light,
Who, when fully assured that a system of religion is unsound,
So veil their dissent under cautious conformity,
That never is the plain faith of their hearts avowed?
Many compromises of practice may be needful,
For the sake of those around us, in a choice of difficulties;
Long may be the diffidence and caution of the young;
But to pass through life, after the judgment is fixed,
Permanently hiding away one's deliberate belief,
Is to abandon our task as servants of truth,
And must grieve God's Spirit and overcloud our own mind.
Those who have least to endure, and least need valour,
Are called on to be foremost; nor may one lay down for another,
How much of ill-will he shall voluntarily encounter.
But there are limits to suppression, which if you outstep,
You become false to yourself, false to mankind:
And as death for conscience' sake has been a high duty,
So *some loss* for conscience' sake may easily be ours,
And the man cannot love truth, who resolves to endure *none*.
Oh, if you prize virtue; oh, if you worship God;
Detest the idea that any riches or preferment
Can compensate a dissembler for a debasing slavery,
Which stamps on him feebleness and secret self-contempt.
Let each therefore judge himself, as surely God judges him.
    Learn rather that it is an honour not dearly bought
To endure reproach, exclusion and partial poverty,
In the noble cause for which ancient martyrs died,—

---

* "Martyr" is the Greek word for Witness.

Martyrs for truth, even when their notions were erroneous,
Since they chose ghastly death, rather than be false at heart.
To be added to their band is generally a cheap honour now,
And is fruitful of good, if truth only is our aim.
For he who cheerfully suffers loss for truth,
Defying the opinion of his immediate public,
Not being soured in mind nor possessed by vanity,
Removes the main obstacles which keep good men dark,
Prejudice, habituation, and wrongful fear of man.
And fearless steadiness gradually wins respect;
So that the faithful confessor of truth gets ever stronger,
And imparts some strength to the more wavering also.
Often is it seen, that high talents are feeble,
For want of a fearless and downright conduct;
While the man who is faithful to his light and brave,
Grows clearer in judgment, purer in discernment,
Larger in heart, and stronger for every good work.

PERFECT AND IMPERFECT VIRTUES.

While the soul is winning a virtue, it is in frequent struggle;
And in the grandest natures the struggle is sometimes greatest:
For every part of man is for service, and all our instincts are good.
It is well that the passions be strong, as well as the desires and affections,
If only mind, conscience and soul be firm enough to guide them.
Nor is that the noblest nature, in which the animal man is puny;
But *that* is noblest, in which all elements are strong and all in harmony.
In the mightiest soul may often be the stiffest battle.
When Passion is stubborn to its bent, but the Mind is steeled to conquer.
Such a soul gets many a wound and carries many an old scar,
Though it win a noble victory and bring on itself no dishonour.
  Yet while the struggle lasts, it is war and not peace;
The victory is about to be won, but it is not won as yet;
The virtue is militant, not triumphant;
It is imperfect, even if soon to be perfected.
But there are many battles, which are not to last for ever.
All the appetites and passions which bring *pleasure* may be tamed and can be tamed,
Until they become servants and faithful soldiers of their conqueror,
And fight under his standard, and rebel or mutiny no more.

Then the virtue is perfect, and the soul thus far is in harmony,
Obedience is without struggle, and even is pleasant,
For the lower nature has become loyal, and is happy in subjection.
Up to this point is Perfect Virtue attainable to man,
And *such* perfection will one day be a common attainment,
Expected of all good young men and taken for granted.

Far different is the case with other sorts of virtue.
"Bear and forbear," was the precept of ancient wisdom:
To forbear is not always a finite task, and to bear is infinite.
To *forbear* from pleasure, may be easy; from anger, difficult:
Also to forbear from harsh words, which are deserved, but unprofitable,
Or unsuitable from *us*, or certain to carry us too far.
Pain cannot be pleasant, nor can uneasiness ever be made easy,
And where is pain and distress, there is more or less of struggle
And some strain on the soul, so that it has not divine repose;
Thus neither can its virtue attain divine perfection.
When affection is wounded by the death of one beloved,
Or wounded morally by his unkindness or unvirtuousness,
To bear the sorrow wisely is never without struggle:
Nor to bear men's unreasonableness and injustice and petulance,
Or to bear hardship and want, and live laborious and contented.

No eye but God's eye knows the virtues of the humble poor,
Of harshly treated servants and of many who linger in sickness,
And of daughters or wives who to the sick are ministering angels.
Wonderful often is their virtue, and by the force of long habit
Toil ceases to distress them and ill-treatment seems not to irritate.
Almost might one think that such virtue had become perfect,
Where habit and affection and sweet cheerfulness soften hardship.
And to the multitude of mankind the reach of highest virtue
Is from the self-denials of affection in the heart of family life,
Or from the self-denials of obedience to superior command,
With contentment and gentleness and thanksgiving to God.
Single acts of heroism, noble and heart-filling,
Are performed often by common men, whom we had not guessed to be virtuous
Yea, by many who (to our knowledge) do not aim at virtue in general:
But the spur of some high moment exalts their goodness;
Nor might their virtue last long, though in short struggle it is glorious.
The long trial of life is the real test of attainment.

Want of leisure and press of duty, concerning which there is no choice,
Keep the multitude engaged in a routine of life;
Nor is their mind widened by knowledge, nor can their aims reach far:

No *ambitious* virtues can seduce them, and their path is plainer.
But those who abound in Leisure, with wealth or knowledge,
Are open to new virtue and to much new vice.
How to bestow free time, is a problem for each to answer
According to his means and capacity and bent;
And therein Selfishness has wide room to lead astray.
Those who have grown strong, are bound to higher tasks,
And, when the Good has become easy, to pursue the Better,
And to find *what is* their task, and perform it manfully.
High duties require labour, or at least permit not ease:
Yet many brave men and women have devoted themselves wisely,
Earning a virtue which to the outward eye is without blemish,
Though we know it could not be perfect nor its battle cease,
Unless man's flesh could become iron and his heart a millstone,
And weariness never oppress his body and mind.

   The purer is man's conscience, the higher is his thought of Duty.
Duty is a taskmaster, who prescribes endless work;
And the higher Virtue rises, the more she herself aspires,
That Right Sentiment, everywhere and alway, may be in ascendancy;
That the love of God be ardent and kindliness to man unfeigned,
And Religion rule the heart and the heart fill the life.
Such virtue is infinite, and never fully to be won,
Always imperfect and often self-reproaching,
Bathed with weeping regrets, and longing for self-sacrifice,
Not to pamper sanctimonious pride nor to mortify the flesh,
But to be able to do more good and to win to the love of goodness;
Or to establish the Right among men, and remove the traps of Ruin,
And elevate us and adorn us and strengthen us and ennoble us.

   Who shall speak fitly of that virtue, sublime though imperfect,
The virtue of the hero-saint, hidden, yet visible to the open eye,
For the good of others resolute and surrendering its all,
Large-hearted to imagine, vigilant to act, unwearied to persevere?
It is sorrowful, yet alway rejoices; humble, yet very confiding;
Aware of human ignorance, yet bold to track divine mysteries.
It exists not save in the deep of soul and patient of thought.
It thrives with man's whole nature,—intellect, fancy, conscience,—
And dwindles with the cramping of genius or narrowing of knowledge.
Therefore its diffusion is for future ages or future worlds,
When mutual love and prudence shall better conspire,
And the lack of one shall be supplied by the riches of many.

MORAL CONTAGION.

The sick sheep is driven away by the rest of the flock,
Lest haply its breath be a pestilence or its touch infectious.
The bird released from captivity, which has forgotten wild instincts,
Is persecuted by its fellows, lest it propagate the forgetfulness.
No weak or crippled brute finds mercy or pity with its species;
For strength is their Virtue, and to be infirm is a Vice.
    Wild man also is inly spurred to stop the progress of contagion,
The contagion of deadly disease, the contagion of evil example,
The contagion of cowardice or of disobedience to the chief.
Wise barbarians forbid the contagion likewise of vice,
Whatsoever ruins the body or defiles the domestic hearth.
They disgrace the drunkard, and scourge the adulterer;
They hang the harlot, and drown abominable profligates.
They forbid traffic in fiery drinks, and banish the traffickers.
When Priest and King join against wine, drunken tribes become sober.
All early religion bids the rulers to stay public immoralities;
All simple nations feel that law is founded on morals,
Else it were not sacred, nor could righteously punish,
Nor could claim to be God's ordinance, or give dignity to the magistrate,
Thus early law is moral, and aims to extend morality,
And honours virtuous marriage, and disgraces its neglect,
And roots up traffic in sin, which is a contagion of deadly ruin.
Under such law weak peoples grow mighty, and the pious intelligent,
Though philosophy still be infantine, and religion superstitious.
    But when through the advances of knowledge superstition is undermined,
And national creeds fall asunder and dissent is common,
And with wealth and prosperity manners become pampered and corrupt,
And traffic in vice brings revenue and convenience to the rulers,
And superstitious fears vanish, and no truer religion takes root:
Then practical atheism domineers in every affair of State,
And the theory grows up that Expediency alone rules in Politics,
That the State is unmoral, and citizenship a mere joining of stock,
And that it befits not the law to take cognizance of vice and sin.
This is one way by which moral rule is disorganized,
And State, King, Law, are desecrated and undermined.
    Or it may be, the rulers stop not at checking public vice,
That which universal conscience pronounces to be crime or sin;
But they will forbid honest inquiry and ingenuous doubt,
And repress mental speculation and the noble pursuit of truth,

And punish novel opinions, and burn the bodies of the faithful.
Then unless the whole mind of the nation can be stunted,
Men's conscience is shocked at the cruel injustice,
And an outcry is made to restrict the sphere of the ruler;
And honest haters of bigotry put forth the deadly doctrine,
That law is unmoral, and may not punish immorality;
That magistracy is public lackeydom, to do things convenient,
As a popular menial, to pave, sweep, and light the streets,—
To tax, to fine, to imprison, to scourge, enslave or hang;
Having nothing moral, nothing religious; and *therefore* may not persecute.

Never shall England be righteous and wise, until this error is unlearned;
Until, as of old, it is understood that magistracy is sacred,
That public life should be pure as private, or even purer,
That law must prevent, rather than punish, crime otherwise abounding,
Must stop vicious contagion and traffic in sin,
And make morality its first aim, wealth its second.
Thus shall vice be stopped from without, and virtue grow up from within.

FOUNDATION OF THE STATE.

When we are able to do good, to do it becomes a duty;
Thus to POWER is attached many moral obligations.
And wherever high Power is held permanently by any,
If GOODNESS be joined with it, it avows subjection to duty,
And is acknowledged also by the weaker as *Ruling*.
WISDOM likewise is needed, with Goodness and Power,
To make the rule of these wholly beneficial:
And if all three endowments could exist in high degree,
Then the rule would indeed seem supernatural and divine.
God is our Ruler, because he is powerful, wise and good:
Man, when powerful, becomes a ruler, even if not wise and good:
But wisdom and goodness make the rule welcome,
Nor can it be long ere it will be felt as legitimate.

To see the germ of *State*-power, consider how men deal with children.
If a man, strong and thoughtful, see two children quarrelling,
And one child is ready to do deadly harm to the other,
The man will interfere and will separate them by force,
And will hinder the harm and rescue the weaker child,
Whether the children consent, or consent not, to his arbitration.

No compact has been made, direct or implied;
Yet his forceful interference is right and justified,
Because his service is needed and there is none else to do it.
So, in a wild country, without institutions of law,
Where otherwise would be anarchy and unchecked outrage,
Honest men who have strength and weapons and power of movement,
Combine in some fixed compulsory organization,
Whether as a republic or under some honoured chief,
To suppress public crime and supply public needs.

 Violence to the person, robbery and theft,
Are doubtless the offences which first and chiefly demand repression.
Yet dream not that these contain the whole duty of the State,
Or that the immorality of crime is no reason for punishment.
The worst offences are offences, expressly because immoral.
Murder and robbery are therefore everywhere punished:
And other doings also, widely different from these,
Which tend to public corruption, are punished in all wise States;
Sometimes with the greatest severity admissible for any crimes.
When deeds confessedly immoral are left without penalty,
It is either because the whole nation is too corrupt for the law,
Or because the lawmaker has a weak sympathy with offenders,
Or because it might lead to tyrannies worse than the offence,
Especially when it is hard to define the immorality.
Seduction of woman is unpunished, if the lawmakers foresee their sons' guilt;
And they punish gambling the more feebly, when many of themselves are gamblers;
And they do not punish ingratitude, because it cannot be defined.
Yet never will Law and Government be therefore held not *moral:*
Pre-eminently moral is its nature and its essential effort.
To promote virtue in the citizens is in truth its fittest aim,
Though disguised by bigots and by the war against bigotry.
Error has imagined that ancient tales are religion,
That such religion is morality, and that its denial is punishable:
Others, in reply, have denied that immorality is punishable,
Which is against all history, all fact, and all reason.
Let confessed immorality be punished, more appropriately than hitherto,
This above all things shall aid us toward a purer state,
But never shall prove that historical doubt is immoral,
Or that to punish the search after truth can be other than tyrannical.

LOYALTY AND ALLEGIANCE.

After the rape of the Sabines, or of the wives for Benjamin,
The captured damsels were nothing but slavish concubines;
And could they have escaped even by fierce violence,
All would sympathize with them and applaud their deed,
So long as the relation was that of unwilling slave,
Unsoftened by conciliation and unsanctioned by mutual pledge.
But if, through despair of a better lot, or won by blandishments,
They accept affection and learn to love in turn,
Then from mutual trust rises mutual Loyalty,
And fit Allegiance between husband and wife;
But the violences of the past are blotted out and buried.

Nearly such is the case with many peoples toward their rulers,
Who by foreign or mercenary armies have trampled them down;
Yet, if afterward the rule be just and equitable,
And the conquered are admitted into manly equality,
Generally will the nation forget or forgive the past,
When the doers and the sufferers of the violence are dead.
Those who have been born in the newer state feel what they *are*,
But less concern themselves to reflect what their fathers once *were*.
If their pride be still hurt and their manliness offended,
By a rule which depresses their noblest and ablest men,
This will gall them as a palpable fetter of the conquest,
And may utterly prevent any sense of Loyalty.
Terrible is such a relation to subjects and to rulers alike,
A baleful curse entailed on posterity by old violence,
When the rulers dare not conciliate the ruled.
Yet if there be no exclusions for race or religion,
And conquered with conquerors become blended in society,
One citizenship unites them in a moral Loyalty,
And the nation embraces the rule as Legitimate and as Its Own.

To be well ruled is a good thing; to be ill ruled is a bad thing;
Yet to be ruled by one's rightful ruler is better than to be well ruled,
And we wish not to be well ruled by a protector not our own.
So feels every woman, and so feels every nation.
The damsel torn from her family, while the rape is fresh,
Resents her captor's blandishments, and scoffs at his "protection,"
If he vow that he will protect her better than any other man;
For she claims a *rightful* protector, one who is *her own*,
Far more than one who will be strong and wise or kind;

And rather would she have a husband of her choice, lord of her heart,
Though he were less wise and strong, and not always even kind,
Than a violent lord who forsooth professes to rule wisely.
So too, if in some evil moment France and Russia could combine,
And should oppress England suddenly by twofold invasion,
And should overthrow our royalty and impose a new rule,
Maintained round our necks by foreign forces;
If in every castle we saw French and Russian soldiers,
French or Russian magistrates in every city, town and village;
It would bring nothing of comfort to be told that their rule was good,
More wise, impartial, energetic than the rule of the old dynasty.
Even if this were true, we should bitterly disdain such blessing,
Feeling neither thanks nor loyalty for a usurper's favours;
But should know our right and duty to expel force by force,
In the very first crisis which might give hope to our efforts.
Such as is English nature, such is human nature everywhere,
Nor can there be Loyalty, till hurt feelings have been appeased.
To conquer, is generally a greater or a smaller crime:
To inherit a conquest, is a direful perplexity.
But a first duty of the heir, if he cannot disown the heritage,
Is to appease, to conciliate, to soothe just resentments,
To honour patriotism and give it a noble field,
So as to enlist true patriotism on the side of Loyalty,
And make Allegiance possible to the virtuous.
Until this is achieved, the best rule is but barbaric,
Forcible, hollow, transitory, bound by no moral band.

PATRIOTISM.

That voice of many peoples, which is a voice of God,
Has in every age and country extolled Patriotism;
A virtue widely diffused in unhonoured multitudes,
Yet needing rare occasions to make it eminent in one man;
Chiefly those of calamitous times, when under mighty foreign force
A people is oppressed, but vainly struggles to unite itself;
Until some heroic leader, winning their confidence,
Combines their action and achieves deliverance,
Often by some violent deed of sudden slaughter,
(As many a time in Israel, and many a time in Greece,

And many a time also in modern Europe,)
When in no other form can war be initiated,
And when the war in itself is rightful and honourable.
Or, when that commonest of tragedies is enacted,
That a prince violates the trust reposed in him by his country,
And overturns the laws by the power given to sustain them,
And calls resistance Treason, and slaughters the innocent:
Then perhaps one or many stand up on the side of right,
Imperilling life and fortune and sacred honour,
And in the name of the nation and of law and of liberty
Rise up against the prince to re-establish lawful rule.
Success in such an effort is praised in every land,
Is honoured in history, and by the severest moralists;
Yet success would be impossible, if no one might act
Without being first secured that action would be successful.
Mere success cannot justify, if the deed beforehand was wrong;
And if beforehand it is right, it is justified without success.
Nothing can result but feeble and selfish conduct
And unjust judgment, to the worshippers of success.
That Patriotism may exist, it must be based on principle.

 A *Nation* is often a real and sharply defined body,
Self-recognizing as a *Family*, conscious of mutual duty,
Of mutual affection and of mutual right;
In so much that to lay down even life for its safety
Is an ordinary sacrifice, expected from common men,
A sacrifice nobly made by untaught and homely virtue.
What a world of meaning lies hid in that simple fact!
What a depth of value in the idea of Nationality!
What more can a son do than die for his mother?
Yet common men are expected to die for their country:
And without such Patriotism no nation could long be safe,
Neither in possessions, nor in persons, nor in laws, nor in religion.—
To undervalue this virtue is to undervalue the State itself,
And stability of law and all manly freedom.

 There are times and countries where confusion has so long reigned,
That good men differ what ruling power is lawful;
And where doubt is wide-spread, to treat it as Treason is tyranny.
There are other cases where Insurrection is a sacred right or duty,
As to which sound Morality is clear and unhesitating:
Where it is manifest that the Power which claims dominion
Does not govern a country, but occupies it with war;

When armies overawe everything, suppressing civil courts,
And leaving no rule to equitable and even law,
But mis-governing on system, by soldiers, spies and constables;
Chiefly if they be armies of foreigners, and if in all high office
Mere foreigners domineer, striving more for power than for right.
Cruel and terrible is the guilt of choosing such a posture,
Which stirs up to rightful resistance the hearts of true patriots,
And makes war on Nationality, a name dear and sacred
As the name of wife and mother to every sound-hearted man.—
But alas! great empires yield not even rights to fellow-men,
And need many deep sufferings yet* to teach them Justice.

STATE PUNISHMENTS.

No man of sound mind will disparage morality
Merely because *morals* have grown up out of *customs*.
In the order of history so has God ordained,
That wild Instinct comes first and tempering Reason follows,
Not creating, but forbidding, selecting and guiding.
Out of Instinct arise Customs, many of them pernicious:
But Custom chastened by Reason engenders Morals,
And morals attain ripeness by the collision of diverse nations.

Nor will any sound mind disparage State-punishments,
Although they were at first deeds of high-handed caprice,
As we see among savage tribes; where the priest and chieftain
Are sometimes of accord to punish sin and crime justly,
But sometimes gratify pride and insolent ferocity,
And stir their warriors to crime under pretence of punishing.
But the rule of Law at length terminates Caprice;
And Law which is even to all, is dreadful to all if unjust;
Hence its injustices become corrected in all nobler races.

If the State did not punish, no growth of Law were possible,
Nor any steady advances in national morality,
Nor permanent elevation of a people, nor much of individuals.
State-punishments are manifestly right, and none dare to blame them;
Yet some who deprecate forfeiture of life, so reason against it,
As to reason against all public penalties whatsoever;
While they urge that it grew out of the uncontrolled ferocity of chieftains,

---

* Written in 1857.

Out of merciless caprice and self-willed pride.
Such reasoners otherwise also betray hatred of all punishment:
For if *scourging the body* be proposed, they make outcry,
Saying that it is torture, and torture is not punishment,
But is barbarous and hardening, and demoralizes even spectators,
And unteaches compassion and prepares for crimes of violence.
And if *hard labour* be proposed, that they deprecate as unequal,
As cruel to the weak of body and nothing but slow torment,
And producing hatred of industry, and thus demoralizing.
To *transportations* and to all *exile* they have valid or strong objection,
And to *punishment of the purse* they avow animosity,
As enabling the rich to revel in crime at a price easy to him,
While it falls severely on the more tempted poor man.
And in *imprisonment* they find evils direful and unjust:
For, solitary imprisonment breaks the spirit and makes men idiots,
And social imprisonment depraves the less criminal by the worse,
And taints all as with pestilence, and ruins after-reputation,
Even to those whose virtue may have escaped utter wreck.—
Evidently then, if we would not explode all punishments entirely,
Of punishments, as of taxes, we must be contented with the least hurtful.

There are other men, wise and cautious, who in comparing valid penalties,
Disapprove life-forfeit in the ordinary code of peace,
Not because wrong in itself, but because not the best of punishments.
To reason against such, belongs not to this place:
Nay, perhaps they are quite correct; I mean not to gainsay them;
Opinion inclines that way, not in one nation only but in many.
But it is suitable nevertheless to protest here and enforce,
That to punish by scourging, by mutilation or by killing,
Is for some offences justifiable, and compassion is there out of place.
In fact, this is visible in every extreme case,
As when robbers or mutineers behave as maniacs and as devils.
To destroy them, until they are disarmed, is our duty,
And *so* to punish the most guilty, as to deter others from like crime.

What form of punishment may most deter imitators,
Must depend in part on the sentiments of a people:
But whichever will most deter, *that* is most merciful,
If crime be great, liable to spread, and a source of vast misery.
Nor, where the cruelty and outrage have been deep and horrible,
Can strict retaliations be forbidden by Justice,
As, to torture the torturer; though Expediency may forbid;
For, Experience apparently limits the infliction of pain to simple scourging,

And infliction of Hunger on fierce criminals may subdue the proud spirit enough.
Also, it is often true that the mere destruction of the guilty,
(Though it be a partial removal of a pest,) deters but little,
Since it is quickly forgotten, just as loss of life in war.
Then to deter, most fitting is some permanent mutilation,
(So have all Orientals and the old Romans known,)
As, to lop off the right-hands of bands of murderers,
Turning them adrift to beg their bread anywhere,
And display to millions the penalty of direful guilt.
It belongs not to this place to discuss the Expedient,
But to avow that where crime has been extreme and hideous,
Penalties of this nature, permanent and visible,
Inflicted, not promiscuously, but on actual convicts,
Are Righteous and Merciful, fit to be used upon occasion.

Most persons discern all this, when confronting widespread horrors,
But they want imagination to preconceive such horrors;
And they shriek against the cutting short of ten or twelve guilty lives,
Unable to foreshape what a growth of guilt it prevents.
He indeed who has once poisoned with success and with impunity,
Becomes an adept in poisoning and is hardened in his art;
But violent murder unchecked becomes both a habit to one man,
And a league of crime to many; and engenders brigandage,
Which has to be put down by war and by massacre,
With loss of many good lives beside those of the guilty.

But what is most strange in some men's spurious mercy,
Is their reasoning from the doctrine of Immortality.
They would not wish guilty souls to be hurried into judgment,
Before time has been given to repent of their evil deeds!
Were there no future judgment, they would more lightly kill!
Thus they deprecate not *death*, but distrust God,
And suppose him to be less merciful and less just than we are!
To reason with such superstition is probably hopeless,
Yet we will briefly protest, that in removing an inveterate murderer,
We take a life most worthless here on earth,
Worthless to the individual equally as to society.
For, base and aggravated murder makes after-virtue impossible;
And to be removed from earth is best for any man,
When he can no longer be a trusted inmate of the human family.

And why is human life to be respected as sacred?
Not because it is given by God; for so is the life of beasts.
Not because the soul is immortal; this can but lessen the loss of life.

But clearly because the man is a moral existence,
A fraternal member of the human family.
When he no longer can claim to be within this description,
His life becomes cheaper than that of a useful beast.
 Nevertheless, there is a second side to this dreadful subject,
Without which all here written on Punishment may laboriously miss the mark.
We must therefore proceed to speak on the Prevention of Crime.

PREVENTION OF CRIME.

 When one child in a family is notorious for wickedness,
He is to the parents a disgrace as well as a sorrow:
For from wiser training better result might be hoped;
So great is the power of adult over tender minds.
The same judgement with equal truth applies itself to nations,
That to them also it is an infamy to abound with criminals.
If crime pervades all orders, probably the whole people is corrupt,
Too vicious to bring a remedy to its own diseases,
Though in time they may be outgrown, if they belong to mere early barbarism.
But if the higher ranks have intelligence and some virtue,
With nothing of fierce crime and reckless brutality,
And affect to be civilized and humane and just;
Then to such it is a brand of shame before God and man,
If brutality and crime be wide-spread in the lower orders.
For, these latter, like to mere animals or helpless children,
Are in great measure the creatures and the sport of circumstance,
Which forms their habits and limits their character,
As is testified by the monotony of countenance, sentiment and mind:
And those who are entrusted with intelligence and government,
Those who enjoy wealth and leisure by the toils of the many,
Are despicable and guilty if they apply their leisure to selfishness
And overlook the untrained, who live neglected and debased.
 When institutions have been originally unjust, as imposed by force,
And injustice has been pronounced sacred, and has hardened into rock,
And the ruling classes have forgotten the origin of the institutions,
Or fancy that mere time makes injustices just;
So hard (through the conflicts of opinion) is their removal,
That wealthy refinement finds an excuse for inactive selfishness,
Saying that it disdains political squabbles and endless talk.

Such a nation may need the scourge of abounding crime,
Threatening its daily life and damping its happiness,
To force it into preventing crime as well as punishing.
And when it has been found that punishments, though necessary,
Do but feebly deter, because life is so worthless to the brutalized,
Evidently the right course both for prudence and for mercy
Is to study to make life more valuable to the wretched,
By alluring them to pure pleasures suited to their attainment,
By discouraging those who traffic in their vice,
By seeking fit occasions for the interchange of sympathy,
And breaking up their too exclusive mutual society;
But chiefly by removing everything fundamentally unjust,
In the distribution of God's common gifts, Air, Water and Land.
The task is too vast for individuals unaided by Law,
Yet every public man can do much by word and small example,
And many private men can aid to establish the Faith,
That *to prevent crime* is pre-eminently the duty of the State;
Against that false pernicious doctrine, so powerful to impede,—
Fruit of spurious Economy and spurious "Voluntaryism,"—
Which forbids the dwellings of the poor to be made a public question,
Or the study of their virtue, or the prevention of their pauperism:
Also, against that proclivity of officials, to talk much of Reforming Criminals,
(A task hugely difficult, and of infinite expense)
While of preventing Pauperism and Crime little or nothing is said;
Because, though vastly easier in itself, it would be less acceptable to the powerful.
How such things may be regulated, it is for Politics to discuss:
But let no one think, that, by calling himself a religious man
And affecting to be too spiritual for political duties,
He can shake off responsibilities which are naturally his.
Nay: but true religion will teach him to be a thoughtful citizen,
Studying the public welfare, and not his own table only.

MURDER.

"He who sheddeth man's blood, by man shall his blood be shed."
This ancient utterance in barbarous times was current,
Over the parched deserts of Asia, as amid American forests and savannahs.
It is still held sacred in Europe, and perhaps seems a basis of civilization.
The sentiment at bottom is sound; but the letter, made sacred, has been pernicious.

"If to shed man's blood be alway a crime,
Then he who sheds in revenge of crime is himself a criminal."
So argues now one school or sect of Englishmen,
Who indict the legal hangman as a murderer.
So too argues the Persian Soofie: "If I do evil,
God who does me evil in turn, is no better than I."
The fanatical Englishman is on a par with the skeptical Persian.
As interpreted by the Arab and by the brown man of America,
On the primitive maxim was knit a chain of slaughter.
Bloodshed could only be washed out by bloodshed,
And the retaliation needed ever to be retaliated.
This mischief has continued into recent times,
Wherever the revenge of murder was esteemed a family-heritage;
Thus blood-feuds between tribes became a wide-spread curse.
Yet chiefly to intentional killing was the doctrine applied,
Such as slaughter in open battle, where warriors are face to face.
But the letter of the maxim distinguishes not accident from intention,
Nor momentary passion from malice and premeditation;
Nay, it confounds the reluctant duellist, the disciplined soldier,
With the hired assassin; and if you further press the letter,
It applies not at all to hanging or poisoning where no blood is shed,
Modes of killing less familiar to warlike tribes.
The maxim is but a motto, suggestive of thought;
But possessed of no authority to dictate any general rule.
Wide information, close examination, cultivated reason, alone can dictate.
Through the deplorable inaction of the moral judgment,—
An inaction, which habitual leaning on a sacred authority induces,—
Englishmen, removed from an English public become signally atrocious;
Not through ferocity, but ordinarily through avarice.
So has it been with the Spaniards, so with the Hollanders.
Released from habitual controul, we quickly lose moral perception:
Then neither man nor woman is safe from our passions.
 In nations which abound with freedom and high spirit,
Which also are surrounded by others of doubtful amity;
Such as was the infancy of Europe, and also our Middle Age of barbarism;
In them the very best men might bear the ill-fame of killing.
All needed to be trained to arms, all carried arms habitually;
Sham fights were used in training; sham fights were an amusement;
In the hunting of wild beasts deadly weapons flew variously.
To discriminate accidental slaughter from deliberate was often impossible.
When Sir Walter Tyrrell's arrow slew King William Rufus,

Who could tell whether it was aimed at him or unaimed?
Who should assure King Crœsus whether by purpose or by accident
His son was slain in the boar-hunt by Adrastus' dart?
Because dire suspicion often remained in the kinsmen's hearts,
Therefore, alike in Greece, in Lydia, in Judæa,
Exile was imposed on the accidental slayer;
A foreign soil became his sufficient, but his necessary defence.
Therefore also were asylums appointed, where the slayer was safe,
Until an impartial tribunal might judge of his deed.
The noblest and the bravest were thus liable to exile.
At the funeral of Patrochus, how lightly might Diomedes,
As Homer sings of it, have slain his honoured comrade Ajax!
The keenness of rivalry might then have looked like murder.
Through such possibilities, and such uncertainties of motive,
A pecuniary ransom, with many rude peoples,
As punishment for the slayer appeared to suffice:
Hence actual murder seemed by no means the worst of crimes.
The subject is truly complex; contingencies are manifold.
Five Spaniards in 1528, on the coast of Florida, unskilful in hunting,
Driven by starvation, devoured one another.
First was one sacrificed to the hunger of the four; next a second was eaten by three,
Thus was the process continued, till a single survivor survived;
He survived, as he reported, "only because there was no one to eat him."
The savage brown men who learned of such doings were shocked,
And thenceforward looked at all Spaniards with something of disgust.
But who of us would have hanged the survivor of the ghastly four?
Punishment enough was in dire memory, and in the sense of human abhorrence:
Why should we slay such a man? Is he dangerous to mankind?
Think you that he will prowl for human flesh in the future?
The error of reasoning, is to suppose that Punishment is mere Vengeance,
And looks solely to the past. To judge of moral guilt,
It does look to the past, without which no Punishment is just:
Nevertheless, the aim of Punishment is always at the future.

As to duelling, manifestly our law was in like error,
Where the public conscience never ratified the rulings of judges.
The challenger was generally guiltier than the challenged;
Yet military sentiment and even military codes
Disgraced as a coward him, who, when rudely insulted,
Declined to challenge; nay, and so sensitive was honour,
That an English prime minister, our noblest commander, became a challenger.
But the law accounted death from a duel premeditated *murder*,

And this, whether the challenger or the challenged were slain.
Was it feared that the slayer would slay again, *otherwise* than in a duel?
It was *not* feared: but men's minds were enslaved to the Letter.
Disgrace and heavy fines, would easily have stopt the mischief.
But law was evaded, and was necessarily impotent,
When the gentry and the wealthy sympathized with law-breakers.

Of other kind is our treatment of wronged and miserable womanhood,
Where the wronged woman is generally of a lower class.
When a poor girl is seduced by a scoundrel professing love,
And heartrending shame overpowers motherly instinct,
So that in agony of soul she destroys her new-born babe,
Vainly hoping to hide her loss of woman's honour;
Then the cruel law confounds her deed with murder:
Nay, to ensure conviction, proves the guilt from concealment of birth.
Surely Punishment *enough* is in a mother's dire memory,
Too much in the agony of shame and in the public notoriety.
Why slay such a woman? think you that emboldened by impunity
She will take to the trade of murder and be dangerous to mankind?
Surely to slay her is greater barbarity avenging a lesser.
Again, where sand and rock, or forest and swamp domineer,
Over many scores of miles which interpose wild desert,
Many a time has a travelling company been so pressed for time,
Whether by the elements, by scant provision, or by dread of a foe,
That they dare not abate their violent speed of march.
Then the weakest or the aged falls behind inevitably,
Nor do the strongest of the band avail to carry them.
Life cannot be wholly saved, yet all need not die:
Thus, as in a battle, a part dies to save the rest.
None then will call it murder to abandon the feeble.
What then if the abandoned implore to be rather slain?
What, if the aged father claim of his son's filial duty,
To slay him there, and not leave him to wolves,
Or as food, while alive, to famine and to insects?
Is the son a murderer for piteously obeying the father?
Like cases of hopeless suffering arise among ourselves,
Where relief to the sufferer is refused from dread of murder.
Minds are prepossessed by that ancient formula, concise and cutting:
No reasoning is calmly heard, but outcry and revilings domineer.
Yet a clergyman has lately printed, from long experience in a parish,
That while patients are driven into frenzies by agony,
Their pious kinsfolk pray to God for death,

Pray, that HE will do, what MAN can do and dares not do.
On such a matter surely the opinions of the wise ought to be collected.
Certainly for cases like these, as likewise for hopeless madness,
Never was that sacred formula of ancient men written:
But the question remains fully open, and must receive calm discussion,
In spite of the violence of bigotry, which prejudges and slanders.

   The public sentiment which is thus savage against a seduced woman,
Whose wrongs it stingily redresses, and heartlessly aggravates,
Lets loose armies of murderers and ravagers under colour of the word War,
At the will of a secret cabinet, without misgiving of conscience;
And poisons by compulsion the blood of innocent babes,
Alledging that a healthy infant is a focus of pestilence!
Thus Babes are murdered in England, under sanction of solemn statute,
Enacted in Parliament by persuasion of a medical hierarchy.
So dull of understanding is superstitious Europe,
The slave of routine and of pretended science.

   In the barbarous stage violence comes chiefly from angry passion,
But in the industrial stage the chief fear is from *Avarice*.
Of all ruffian murderers, he who murders for gain is most dangerous,
Expressly because he has *no* "malice prepense" against the victim.
So with him who risks to massacre without troubling himself with thought,
As the contractor who supplies unsound provisions to an army,
Or constructs unsafe bridges or ships, solely to fill his own purse.
So too the reckless mason, who, to leave work after him,
Purposely mars pipes and drains, and fills a dwelling-house with pestilence;
Whence fevers seemingly mysterious, and many a death.
Truly do the moderns need new moral teachings.
Without deeper morality in the many, Murder will not be stayed by Vengeance.

THE TWO-FOLD LAW.

   He is not yet righteous, who only doeth righteous deeds,
But he who doeth them from deliberate choice of righteousness.
Such a man is God's freeman, constrained by no law,
Save by the law of his conscience, which is God's own voice within.
While this law is intelligent, and conscience bears full sway,
Other law is not needed, nor punishments, nor judge,
Nor petty rules of form, and of time, and of place,
Fettering manly discretion and overriding special proprieties.

For, the life that is within will find out all delicate detail,
The rightest place and time and mode for each thing.
But the outward law is general, unexcepting and coarse,
Blind as to everything special, and counting on blind obedience,
The obedience of slaves, not freemen ; of children, not of men.

   The child is too ignorant to be guided by inward discretion ;
The slave of sin and crime is constrained by punishment.
For such the spirituality of religion is not yet a law,
Nor has it any penalties, nor any sufficient training.
The child must be kept under the tuition of the parent,
And slavish-hearted men under the moral training of law.
The law of the land fulfils not its purpose and the ordinance of God,
Unless it be guardian to those who cannot yet have discretion ;
Unless it put down all traffic in sin which corrupts the weak ;
Unless it teach right to the ignorant, and save the outcast from despair.

   The law of the land becomes honourable, when it studies moral aims,
And plants the orphan in families, and trains the untaught to labour,
And fences up the paths of crime, and prevents evil habits,
And cherishes the purity of woman, and watches over the rights of the weak,
And when the innocent are destitute, has a care lest they be made criminal.
Such law is a glory to the land; such law is a blessing from God,
Spreading abroad virtuous habits among the multitude of the ignorant;
Whose virtue is to be industrious and honest and simple-hearted,
Innocent of great offences, and docile to the wiser.
Then, if amid them are found churches which teach a higher doctrine,
And live by the law of the Spirit, in the faith and love of God ;
Quickly will such a people run and listen meekly within the church,
And will learn its best lessons, and practise nobler duties ;
Until the child grows to be a man, by God's Spirit within,
And the bondman is adopted into the full liberty of the freeman.

   If Christians were wise and cared more for goodness than for riddles ;
If with all their heart and might they loved the souls of their brethren ;
They would join heart to heart, hand to hand, voice to voice,
And would claim that the State seek chiefly for moral ends.
They would know their worst foes to be immoral politicians
And all other traffickers in men and women's virtue ;
A slave-trade more hateful than all other slave-trades,—
For here soul and body both together are bought and sold,
While the law-makers look on, and talk about interests and freedom.

   Ah ! Will the Churches ever cry out against real iniquity,
Against seduction of women and against the hell-fire of drinks ?

Will they ever demand that the law shall be moral and the statesmen true?
Or shall their silence and apathy suggest spiritual death,
That God has forsaken them, that they know not his law,
Which is supplanted by forms and rites, by creeds and jargon,
And care not for either law,—whether the law of the land be moral,
Or whether the law of the churches be that of the Spirit?

POMPS AND VANITIES.

All Christendom affects to renounce Pomp and Vanity:
Between Protestant and Catholic there is here no schism.
He who is baptized into Christ, and puts on Christ,
Is buried with Christ to sin and vanity!
"The Pomps and Vanities of this Wicked World"
Are pre-eminently denounced in the Anglican ritual.
Yet what are in truth these Pomps and Vanities,
If not such things as are the life of Sovereigns,
With full sanction of all high dignities in Church and State,
Whose example corrupts a whole nation into vanity?
If any one avow that the theory is erroneous,
Which deprecates Wealth and condemns the lust of the eye,
He is treated as an enemy of divine Truth.
Yet if any one in earnest espouse the theory,
So far as to denounce Pomps and Vanities as evil,
He is scorned as a Puritan, or hooted as a Republican.
Nevertheless, it abides as a certain and dreadful truth,
Attested by Statistics in unsentimental figures,
That in proportion as Courts are brilliant and their Armies gay,
Their pageants numerous, and their drawing-rooms thronged,
Their theatres and their operas and their festivals splendid;
The more do harlots abound, and society becomes rotten,
And crime pervades the life, and whole Classes are Dangerous.
It therefore is not for nothing that Religion has decried worldly pomp,
With foreboding instinct loathing prodigal glitter;
Nor can he who fosters Evil cheat Evil of its prey,
Though he be King or Bishop, or a Soldier hating Puritanism.
Such things are easy for the open eye to understand,
But few, alas! are earnest in the battle against Evil.

Our National Religion is the tool of the richest classes:
What conduces to their honour and convenience, they espouse;
What reproves their darling habits, this they fiercely reject.

LUXURY

He who has many duties needs many aids
Of servants, of clerks, of horses and carriages,
Nor will any one begrudge him the means and skill
Which spare useful time and save high energies;
Though the same means and skill and sumptuous outlay,
When applied to no nobler end than that of living for Self,
Be reproved as Luxury in an ignoble sense.
He in whose hand is vast wealth, blamelessly inherited,
If he apply it to his own ease, without other visible iniquity,
Earns certainly no public praise, and yet but feeble blame,
Blame, less as a citizen, than on religious score:
For his Luxury is thought to harm the man only, not the public.
Nor may this be untrue, while the Luxury is eccentric,
The whim of an individual, not the Object of Life with a class;
But in the latter case it is baneful to the entire community.
For if luxuries are held needful, not to duties, but to rank,
To all born in one class, be they rich or dependent,
Then whatever the style of life with the richest of the class,
Nearly the same is expected of the poorer and of the young.
Then the young men dare not marry virtuous wives, if poor,
And daughters are sold by parents into splendid misery,
And marriage is profaned, and marriage vows are broken,
And wealth becomes an idol shamelessly worshipped,
And fathers tell their sons that profligacy is better than poverty,
And the wealthy become heartless to the sufferings of the poor,
While they live apart in proud ease out of sight of misery;
And class separates from class through the whole nation,
And the poor live in masses, on trades created by luxury,
Liable to suffer from mere vicissitudes of the market
And from the fitful caprices of fashionable demand.
All men know these evils, but most men despair of remedy.
The remedy will come, when the rising generation gains heart
To love virtue more than wealth and more than a parent's smile:

To court as friends whoever are noblest in mind,
To marry for virtue, with or without wealth;
To live in a simplicity which keeps them independent,
Defying the tyranny of fashion and despising the pride of life.
But ere the remedy come thus from within, it may come painfully imposed
    from without.

THE ELECT.

  Shall Religion alway take up but a small part of mankind,
A mere gleaning left to God after Worldliness has reaped the harvest?
That which ought to be to man's soul as light and warmth and food,—
That which is cheap as the light, poured down freely from God,—
Shall it be for ever the portion and privilege of the few?
  Truly this cannot be for ever: long has the faith stood sure,
That righteousness shall spread over Earth and reign over the peoples,
Banishing sin into corners, till it disappears as an insanity.
For as truth conquers Falsehood, so must Right conquer Wrong,
And Religion triumph over Atheism and over all the hosts of Paganism:
For the Better is the Stronger; and the stronger will rule.
Nevertheless every victory has its necessary conditions,
Which those must fulfil who would win the victory.
  We are born into the world, we live and work in the world;
We cannot go out of it, nor choose but breathe its air.
Let spiritual teaching do its best, yet we learn first from mothers,
From nurses, from domestics, from the whole family around us,
From companions and playmates, from fellow-workmen and masters,
From the habits of business and principles of the world.
And as long as the world's atmosphere remains corrupt,
So long will it poison the feeble, the less noble and less fortunate;
And spiritual doctrine comes too late, to purify and to heal,
And wins but a few, and leaves the majority untouched.
The corruptions of one day will undo the preachings of a year,
And traffickers in sin will tempt weakness fatally.
Let virtue in maturity have the spirit of martyrdom,
But from the immature and from learners none may expect this:
And without it, how can a corrupt world be overcome?
When falsehood is made honourable in all high places,
And frauds are current in trade, and despotism exacts cringing,

He who seeks to be virtuous must have a martyr's spirit;
For to be crushed and starved hangs over the unyielding,
Nor can common men afford to keep a conscience.
While this subsists, the virtuous can be but few;
For, sin is strong before virtue's strength can ripen.
Thus the evil and the good of Society are in implacable war;
The good must destroy the evil, or be undermined by it.
The spiritual must resolve to trace mischief to its origin,
And to purify the streams at their higher fountains,
In the family, at the market, in the counting-house, on the farm,
In the shop, the courts, the parliament, the council-chamber.
For while their daintiness abandons the world to its courses,
The world in turn will be a curse on their spiritualism:
So has it always been, and so will it ever be.
As the Church prizes her life within, she must cherish virtue without,
Must attack all pollutions and public sins,
And demand virtue in the law, honour in its guardians,
Truth and plain-speaking and uprightness and justice,
If the kingdoms of this world are to display the judgments of our God.
  The present is child of the past, parent of the future:
What we sow, others will reap; fruit of our sloth or thrift.
Oh dream not, that if ye who should be God's servants are idle,
He will come down with angels to do your neglected work,
Accoutred in kingly pomp, with weapons irresistible,
And so will purge out iniquity from among mankind.
Nay, but on *you* lies the task of purifying the world,
If in any sense or degree ye are the Light or Salt of the earth:
And that Church will best show the earnestness of its faith,
Which sets itself resolutely to root up the *causes* of sin,
Purifying the outward air, and removing traps from the weak.
So and so only shall a Church grow broader and stronger:
So and so only shall the Elect swell into multitude.

POLITICAL EXPEDIENCY.

  Reasoners abound, who would persuade us that Public life
Cannot bow, as Private life, to the sway of Right and Wrong:
Because (say they) the sacrifices which Virtue often claims
Are here on too great a scale to be equitably expected;

And the greatness of a result justifies contempt of a principle.
A private man, who discovers that his dealing is wrongful,
Must withdraw, must apologize, must make restitution:
But if a Great Power has perpetrated a crime,
Has wantonly bombarded a city or destroyed a fleet,
Through passion and petulance or the pride of strength;
The Great Power cannot afford to indulge in repentance,
To confess, to lament, to repay whatever can be repaid;
But must persevere in the evil deed, and plunge deeper into guilt,
Lest it harm its credit by daring to own its wrong.

 This doctrine is whispered perpetually in private circles,
And it unquestionably influences the deeds of statesmen;
Yet rarely, if ever, dare they utter it to the public,
Lest it rouse the indignation of "the stupid good people;"
Nor do they ever endure it as a plea against themselves
On the part of another, that he could not afford to be just;
But they press Treaties against the weak, though violently obtained,
And claim their observance, cost what it may to the other side.
As the old Greek knew neither justice nor mercy to foreigners,
Except so far as Treaty and Oath might have stipulated;
So do these politicians know of no political rights of men,
Until they have been professed and ratified in Treaties.
Then however at least, they acknowledge the law of Right.

 But believe not *thou* that Public life has any rule more true
Than the rule of Right and Wrong, which is supreme in private life.
Believe not that Wrong, by the hugeness of its scale,
Can ever become anything than Wrong more direful.
Believe not that the great virtues of Justice, Truth and Modesty
Can less suit the greatest powers than the very least.

 If ever a Great Power has made a false step
Through the error of its servants and human infirmity;
To confess, to apologize, to restore and to repay
Would come with grace more graceful by reason of its strength,
And would gloriously initiate a real international morality.
The weak and the tottering may in some cases sincerely plead,
That the sacrifices due to virtue would be to them destructive,
And that they cannot afford to consult tender conscience:
Wretched and absurd is the plea; for, if it be a true one,
Then it strictly proves that they have no right to exist.
But a truly Great Power can always afford to be virtuous,
And surely strengthens itself by consistent sacrifices to virtue.

It is not the Great Power, but the foolish and wicked statesman
Who dares not apologize, but prefers to incur fresh guilt.
Such men are the curse of nations and disgrace of Christendom,
A pest to morality both public and private.
To the public they talk plausibly of Justice and Right and Treaty,
But in their dark councils crooked Expediency domineers,
A topic rightful in its place, but not rightful against Justice.
  No statesman dares to enter upon a great war,
Without pretending to his nation that Justice is its ground and aim.
For where great sacrifices, great exertions are needed,—
Where men must step forward to die as willing victims
Or submit to mutilations and to lingering diseases,
Where wives, mothers and orphans must resign their dear protectors;
Even the statesman feels how needful is the high argument,
Which can derive support from a holier Will above us.
But to appeal to God in a war of mere Expediency,
(As if other nations had not their Expediencies also,)
Is felt to be profanity, by the worshippers of a Universal God.
God is a just judge, and favours no special people;
God smiles on no cause but on a Sacred cause,
Nor is mere Expediency sacred, but only the Just and the Right,
Nor is any war defensible, on which we cannot invoke a blessing;
Therefore it must be sacred, and must visibly *so* rest upon the Right,
That the enemy is, and ought to know that he is, Wrong.
This is always pretended in the manifestoes of statesmen;
Who hereby confess that in the *greatest* of national affairs
The Just and the Unjust are clear enough to be paramount.
Never therefore allow crafty pleaders to assume,
That the dealings of nations, "*by reason of their magnitude,*"
Must be judged by other laws than the Right and the Wrong,
When war, the greatest of them all, is to be judged by Right and Wrong.
Nay, but as the stars obey the same laws as the clods of earth,
So no human affairs are too great for moral law.

POLITICAL VACILLATION,

Unscrupulous Ambition often goes straight at its mark,
Trampling down in its course the bodies and souls of men,
Sometimes aiming only at wretched self-aggrandizement,

Far oftener deluding itself by patriotic notions,
By dynastic fanaticism or blind religion.
Those who are moved by passion may be erring, yet are brave;
And moreover their passion may generally be counted on,
Nor does it easily entrap and ruin by vacillation.
Such Ambition may be terrible, but is not despicable,
Except as we pity great powers unworthily applied:
And even when its track is desolating as a hurricane,
It is possibly a high agent for destroying untractable evil.

    Far other is the statesman whose polestar is *Expediency*,
A "polestar" which dodges him in orbits incalculable.
He abhors passion as a frenzy, and he means to be reasonable:
His darling ideal perhaps is moderation and compromise:
Moral principles with him are "unpracticable crotchets,"
And sticklers for the right he calls "cantankerous" and "pedantic."
As a true man of the world, who must behave politely everywhere,
He has torn out of his heart all virtuous indignation
And learnt to smile sweetly on guilt in all high places.
Men who have thoroughly subdued noble and just hatreds,
And have enthroned the spirit of icy materialism,
Disliking enthusiasm as an unmanageable nuisance,
Are habitually timid, vacillating and feeble.
Seldom can they understand the generous movements of nations,
Or even judge how the heart of their own people is set.
At the enmity of any small knot of fanatics, they tremble.
With good intentions, they never know what is right;
For they call the Expedient right; and Expediency ever changes.
Scarcely do they succeed, before they dread to succeed too well,
Lest their allies or their supporters become too powerful;
Lest they soon wish the humiliation of him whom they are exalting,
Or desire the restoration of another whom they are deposing.
Often rash to begin, they always leave off feebly,
And abandon in treaties whatever has been won in war.
Nor can there be any end or limit to their blunders,
Unless they could attain divine foresight of the future.
For he who would guide international affairs by Expediency,
Needs an infinite mind to comprehend unnumbered contingencies;
Else the seeming good becomes evil and the evil good,
When friends turn to enemies and enemies to friends,
As must happen, if each seeks but for his own interest.
Naturally then and rightly these politicians are cowards,

Bullies perhaps of the weak, but cowardly to the strong;
Cowardly to fanatics: false friends to the weak who trust them.
In the high affairs of States, where the happiness of millions is involved,
He alone can be brave, who has a positive ruling passion;
Whether the passion be ambition and strong fanaticism,
Or whether a passionate love of the Right and the Just,
For which man was made, and for which men may die.
Following Expediency, we become cheats, cowards, and fools;
Following Right for Right's sake, we become both brave and wise.

THE ORDER OF PROGRESS.

For flowers and for fruits God has ordained their own seasons,
And each thing comes forward in its proper time and order.
Nor can any skill of cultivator, or any offering of prayer,
Bring the fruit before the flower, or ripe harvest in time of spring.
There are unwise parents, who desire manly minds in children;—
Who grudge to their little ones puerility and sportiveness;
And do not understand, that the child's first task is to thrive,
Growing robust and active and healthy and cheerful.
With such robustness of body gentle minds well suit,
And that unfolding of the intellect which the brain can safely bear:
But all attempts at the premature, we know to ensure failure.

As thus the body grows up earlier than mind and soul,
So its instincts likewise are earlier and more urgent,
Earlier, not to the child alone, but to every human person.
While fierce hunger presses a man, mental instincts are benumbed,
And nature bids him to ravin like a beast for his food,
Postponing spiritual thoughts, the lack of which is less pinching,
Till, the finite appetite being sated, he may have leisure for the infinite.

Whither do we chiefly look for virtue and for moral wisdom?
Seldom perhaps to those, who are overladen with grandeur or wealth,
Yet assuredly far less to those who are extreme in poverty.
The man who is enslaved by work, has no leisure time,
Whether to train his mind to study or his heart to devotion,
Nor often is it in him to bring up his children to virtue:
And though under extreme penury there be found of pure religion
A few glorious examples, yet very few they are.
Dire hardship and penury generally make men hopeless,

Hopeless and improvident, hardy and hard-hearted,
Reckless of their own lives, reckless of others' rights,
Unsympathetic and difficult to win to virtue.
Now when hardship and poverty is universal to a people,
And all their morals have grown up under it,
They may have certain high virtues in the midst of barbarism,
And be truthful, generous and noble, though fierce and revengeful:
But when indigence is hopeless in the midst of wealth and luxury,
Then its power to harden and corrupt grows terrible.
For, in the heart of the ignorant poor, Desire breeds Envy,
And Envy pours into them belief of injustice,
And evil Suspicion follows, and they become untractable.
Such men are hardly approachable by pure religion.
Hence in every most wealthy country, where civilization is old,
Now live thousands upon thousands of dangerous citizens.
Nor in all the world are they anywhere more formidable
Than in the countries which boast to be called CHRISTENDOM.
Let the reader calmly weigh this dreadful and disgraceful fact,
And he will scarcely fail to understand its causes.

 Individual Christians have understood them and avowed them,
And have won honour to the name of Philanthropy.
But hitherto Philanthropy has been the distinction of a few,
Nor ever with us has been incorporate in Religion
As an ordinary complement of every man's duty.
The Churches cannot help being proud of the Philanthropists,
Yet the philanthropic doctrine blends ill with that of most Churches,
Which retain as eternally true what was true for a little while.

 Under the ruthless and sensual empire of the Pagan Cæsars,
To purify the social fountains and stop the occasions of sin
Was a task too enormous to enter an apostle's mind.
So neither was it commanded in their sacred books,
Which do but advise to palliate misery,
Treating it as inevitable under the empire of devils.
Thus Paul and Peter bid look to a kingdom after death,
But abandon the kingdoms of this world as hopeless,
Until Christ descend from heaven in the glory of his Father.
For Patriotism and Philanthropy those times gave no scope.

 Three classes of men impede moral and spiritual progress;—
Preposterous spiritualists, the selfish rich, and hardened politicians,
Who play into each other's hands and sustain evil.
The *first*, talking highly of spiritualism or perhaps of creeds,

Make light of the moral training, which ought to precede,
By industry, by rights, by physical well-being,
By kindly intercourse with the richer in pleasant relaxation.
The selfish rich, who thrive on vice or on injustice,
Or dread every change, lest it bring some inconvenience,
And by resisting all change hinder improvement ;
These men are still guiltier, because more selfish.
But guiltiest of all are *the hardened politicians*,
Who deliberately and knowingly, calculate their course :
Who speculate on votes and prejudices and animosities,
And, to gain their own advancement, stir up evil passions,
Whether national pride and territorial ambition,
Or bigotry, or evil conservatism, or base cupidity,
And mean fear of small taxes and other meannesses.
Such men, dealing largely in trickery and evil influences,
Seldom dare to offend the vicious, nor can promote virtue.

When evil has multiplied through many generations,
Vast is the effort to remove it, nor will one method suit all,
But every place may need its special remedies,
Most by purely local action, a few by foreign help.
But first of all must it be made a precept of Religion
And a precept of Politics, to root up *the causes* of Evil ;
It must become a Creed, that debasement is unnatural,
Is therefore unnecessary, and is surely preventible ;
That is our duty to prevent, and will be our blessing;
That those who promote the body's welfare, aid the mind;
And that the Moral must precede the Spiritual, in national growth,
Though a few, out of immorality, be rescued into Spiritualism.

VITALITY OF SIN.

Virtue in most men grows up with struggles, perhaps convulsively,
Because passions which are lower in worth are strong earlier in time.
Every higher and glorious principle is in promise a Hercules,
Yet the cradle of infant Hercules is beset by monstrous snakes,
Which threaten to strangle him ere his strength can ripen ;—
A fate generally encountered, unless parental care shelters.
Nor was man made for solitude or for solitary self-development ;
But, as virtue begins from forcible Custom, mutually imposed,

So is it trained more perfectly under the wholesome restraints of society.
And when a people advances morally, these restraints are not cast away,
But are made wiser, juster, tenderer, more discriminating,
If the wisest and best co-operate for the general moral welfare.
But if the wisest and best cast away this care and duty,
If they delegate law-making to men whom morally they disesteem,
If they crucify their good sense as though it were a malefactor,
And fight against other good men rather than against Sin;
Who will wonder that Sin displays horrible vitality?

Oh ye who love Goodness, (and none others love God,)
Abandon your civil war, and turn against your true enemy!
Your dogmas may be correct; yet they are a trap and a curse to you,
If ye value them more than that Goodness which makes God Lovely;
If ye take to your hearts and houses bad men who believe them,
And refuse moral union to good men who reject them;
And lay down a new standard of the Good and of the Bad,
Other than that by which ye judge *Jesus* to have been good:—
Whom surely no one ever yet praised for his orthodoxy,
Or accepted as a good man because he believed in himself,
But because of some absolute perception of unpriestly goodness.
But even if, beset by prejudice, entangled by riddles,
Intimidated by authority, ye cannot so far break loose,
As, in judging of men, to fall back on your own first principles;
Yet at any rate, if your dogmas be the Means, and goodness the End,
Beware of subordinating the End to the Means,
Lest God smite your religion with a deadly blast of his displeasure,
And it die, and rot, and be trampled under foot of men.

Since the beginning of the human race, never perhaps was a land
So abounding with pure love of Goodness as our dear native realm;
So full of warm hearts beating with desire for God's blessing,
Hearts that would sacrifice their all to establish God's kingdom.
England has enough *goodness* to strike down Sin mortally,
If she had but knowledge to stop her ears to fanaticism:
And in England is enough *knowledge* to direct her blows aright,
If those who possess it had force of will and moral warmth.
Awake all! sleep no longer! what? when London has ten thousand harlots,
And every year claims for our Jaganaut a thousand victims,
Shall a people that calls itself Christian fold its hands in slumber?
Or shall *we*, forsooth, Christianize insurgent India,*

---

* Written in 1857. In 1873 we provide Indian harlots for our English troops.

While we drug it with the fierce drinks against which Indians protest?
"Physician! heal thyself!" cry the petty kings of Africa,
Pagans, who allow no harlotry to corrupt their manhood.—
Let us *in truth* heal ourselves, rising in the strength of God,
That strength which already abounds in the hearts of England;
Let the good join with *better* or *worse* to extirpate avowed evil,
And five years shall now do more than ever before did fifty,
And perhaps ere long men will doubt of Sin's vitality.

STRENGTH OUT OF WEAKNESS.

" Out of the mouth of babes and sucklings God will ordain strength,
That he may still the enemy and the avenger."
If all who revere these words duly pondered their import,
Each who knows his own weakness might better learn his strength.
But alas! false modesty robs too many of frankness,
Who dread to be eccentric and presumptuous and proud,
If they vent their true sentiments and unveil their moral hatreds,
Their scorn of meannesses, their indignation at injustice,
When the meanness or injustice is smoothly greeted by their elders,
Whose conscience is grown dull by habituation to decorous wrong.
But the strength of righteousness is in truth and plain speaking,
And where truth is not yet attained, yet plain speaking leads to it.
The wilfully wicked are but few even in a wicked world;
But each is deluded by each, each sinner is comforted by each,
And what none plainly condemn seems to each in turn defensible.
It is possible to be outspoken without being immodest,
Even where it involves disapproval of the great and able.
We may feel truly that we are fallible, while avowing present convictions,
Nor needs any so to speak as though his single judgment were a Verdict;
Yet if each spoke frankly, many evils would soon be swept away:
For want of it, statesmen themselves mistake the nation's mind.
Iniquity is strong, chiefly while she can wrap herself in darkness.
Opinion is a great power, so soon as it is expressed,
But unexpressed opinion is no power at all.
Therefore do tyrants seek to smother the expression of opinion.
Therefore also he, who in a free State does not speak for the Right,
Disuses a high power capable of much public service,
And does his part to allow Wrong and Falsehood to prevail.

Opinion, when expressed, acts not merely by inspiring *terror*,
(This is but a narrow and perverted view of Moral Influence,)
But by stimulating the thought of the well-meaning but apathetic,
And winning (if it be correct) the judgments of thousands.
All men value and desire the good opinion of the rest;
And though they can afford to despise fanatical reprobation,
They will not for ever despise well-grounded disapproval.
Take away from your condemnations animosity and party heat,
Love goodness and God and good men and the right,
Palliate every crime and sin so far as truth will allow,
And your protests against evil shall come with tenfold weight.
For, the Conscience of mankind is fundamentally loyal to the Right,
And when carried astray by lower passion, still rallies to truth,
If addressed by a clear voice speaking with pure motives.
Where the voice and the press are free, so far as law can make them,
The soldiers of righteousness must not say that they are helpless:
Let them show their true colours, and they will soon find their strength.

LAWFUL OBEDIENCE.

When solemn inquest is made concerning a deed of crime,
And judges are gathered under oaths to sacred Right;
If the accused have due notice and rightful hearing,
And all forms be observed as by those who seek for Justice,
And there be no suspicion of malice or levity;
Then, if a grave verdict be announced, with sentence of law,
Man's Conscience is satisfied, and the sentence is held sacred,
Though it deal with the high question of human life;
And the officers of law may carry out the sentence,
Receiving it at second hand, without scruple or hesitation:
Else must the executors of every act re-judge the judgment,
Nor could Justice be enforced at all, if that were needed.
He who obeys lawful power in its ostensibly moral action,
Does not abdicate Conscience or become a tool of evil,
But is a rightful co-operator to a sacred purpose.

But if no forms whatever were used in aid of Justice,
If the accused were not summoned nor his defence heard,
If no effort were made for an impartial tribunal,
If no oath or pledge to Justice were taken by the judges,

If by pleas wholly extraneous a verdict were solicited,
If the judges professed to decide from special interest,
Not on grounds of general justice appropriate to the case ;
Or if rage and haste and popular frenzy prevailed ;
If appeal to law were rejected in favour of Party :—
Surely we could not then justify the executors of the sentence,
If it enacted injustice or extravagant revenge :
But they would abdicate Conscience, wrongfully and wickedly,
Becoming accomplices and tools in robbery or murder.

   So also if a State has quarrel with another State,
And seeks a verdict from an arbitrating tribunal,
Or, where arbitration cannot be, yet aims to be impartial,
And calls an assembly, and pleads for even Justice,
And for Justice' sake desires both sides to be heard
With publicity and gravity and caution and mature thought,
Avoiding cupidity and ambition and party-spirit ;
If this solemn assembly, pledged by oath to decide upon the Just,
Pronounce verdict against the other State, to be enforced even by War ;
Then, should war be decreed, the war ostensibly is lawful :
And though by human infirmity it may still be unjust,
Yet we should exculpate the army which executes the sentence ;
Nor might we condemn it as guilty of abdicating Conscience,
When it yields obedience and seeks not to judge the case.

   But when the rulers of one State have quarrel with another,
And desire no arbitration nor impartial verdict,
Nor form a Court of Justice and exact oaths of Justice,
But shun public discussion and defining of the Right ;
And if they call a Cabinet or a Council or a Parliament,
Plead " reasons of State " and of national Interest,
Invite deliberation on the Expedient, not upon even Right,
But talk of Patriotism as before Justice,
And explode pleas for the Just as unpatriotic,
Or as untruth to one's Party and inconvenient to those in power ;
While no judicial forms and oaths or pledges are enforced :—
Then assuredly the war which is decreed under such auspices,
(As that which is decreed secretly by personal will,)
Has no ostensible mark of being righteous and sacred,
Nor can the public vote discharge private conscience.
But the army which executes a war thus decreed,
(If its grounds be unjust or its measures extreme),
Is but a band of murderers and direful robbers,

Tools of tyranny under solemn pretences.
Never will high success make their obedience lawful,
Nor can any declaration of the war lessen its wickedness.
War which is not Sacred, is execrable crime,
Piracy, murder, robbery on huge and horrible scale.

DEFENSIVE WAR.

He who is suddenly assailed with deadly weapons,
Needs no arbitration, nor can wait for process of law;
But he repels force by force; and if the assailant be slain,
The slaughter will be justified, as in needful self-defence.
Just such is Defensive War, rightly understood.
If another commits a violent deed, or prepares violence,
Which must be resisted by us at once, because time presses;
If he invades a province, or occupies a castle,
Or builds a battery and brings up artillery;
Even if he have slain no one, and plundered no one,
Yet he is preparing manifest violence, and must expect violence.
  A defensive war is not always a war of justice;
For a robber acts in defence, to save his stronghold;
Yet to root up the castles of pirates is just,
And to destroy the fleets with which they commit atrocities.
Nor is this less true, when the pirate is pre-eminently great,
And reigns over millions, and is called Emperor or Queen.
But, so long as barbarism shall domineer in Christendom,
Confounding in one aspect wars just and unjust,
They whose soil is assailed will always think their war to be just.
Now, expressly because, in the absence of Sacred Verdict
Which might satisfy men's consciences and justify aggression,
We do and we must applaud repulse of an aggressor;
Expressly for that reason every aggressive movement
Carries lawlessness on its face, even if it be substantially right,
And it needs elaborate justification with sharp defining of its purpose.
Therefore also it is abomination to leave its moral grounds obscure,
And to wrap in State-mystery the ends aimed at.—
What cannot be proclaimed openly, will do the world no good.
  Confusion and darkness, terrible and fatal,
Has come unawares over War from learned writers,

Who, seeking charitably to soften War's cruelties,
Have taught us to treat both belligerents as honourable,
And to crush our natural horror at unscrupulous ambition.
But one side is always Wrong, and generally both.
Vain also is the excuse, that Offence is but Defence,
When pleaded by him who assumes the initiative of violence,
Unsanctioned by arbitration or by verdict high and pure.
But alas! though Christian priests consecrate our colours,
And with solemn prayer commend each regiment to God,
Not yet do English Christians understand the sacredness of War,
But prostitute its weapons to be tools of secret cabinets,
For the service of conquest, of party, and of dynasties.

MILITARY OATHS.

If some wild rover collect a band of followers,
And forming them into a company, administer solemn oaths,
That they shall follow him and obey him, though he command deeds of violence,
And shall be true to his standard, before God and man :—
No one moderately thoughtful imagines such oath to be binding,
Or that it can ever clear the bandits from a charge of guilt:
Rather, the oath itself is deemed guilty and execrable.
  But wherein does this differ from a despotic Tartar Khan,*
Or from a despotic President, to whom armies have sworn obedience?
Whether a bandit chief or an emperor command an outrage,
Outrageous it abides, nor can the wrong be made right;
Nor will voluntary oaths justify the soldiers more than the bandits
In laying conscience aside, and executing a wicked order.
  It is never the oath that can justly move a soldier,
Nor national spirit, nor patriotism and loyalty;
But only his own conviction that he is a minister of righteousness,
Warring for the right side, as a servant of God.
Most men feel this conviction in repelling force from their own land,
And likewise in other cases, which touch the national conscience.
But where the cause of war is too complex for popular judgment,

---

  * In the formal coronation of Quineh Khan, the Tartar chiefs said to him : "We wish, we pray, we command, that you have power and dominion over us all." Quineh replied : "Are you resolved, each of you, to do all that I command, to come when I call, to go whither I send, *and to kill all whom I shall order to be killed?*" The chiefs replied : "Yes."
  This does but state explicitly what is expected and exacted of every English soldier.

Too obscure in its ground, its aims, and its chances;
As, a dynastic war waged upon foreign soil,
A war for commercial rights based upon treaty,
A war to conquer some foreign or Pagan nation,
Or a war against our own discontented colonists,
(And of such wars as these, Christian History is full,)
In such cases, I say, it is an outrageous iniquity,
Without processes of Justice, to expect soldiers' obedience.
To train men to obey absolutely the word of command,
So as suddenly to attack a nation previously friendly,
When ordered by their officer, who has secret instructions;—
Is to train them to become tools of ambition, piracy and treason.
For what if he choose to act the freebooter on his own account,
Trusting that "accomplished facts" are sure to be accepted,
And feign secret orders, or misinterpret or disobey?
Or what, if the head of the Executive plot usurpation?
The men have been accustomed to lay aside all conscience,
To ask no questions concerning Right or Law,
And to obey the commanding officer unconditionally and promptly,
However ruthless and unexpected may be the deed commanded.
This very vow made by Jesuits to the General of their Order,
Has been reprobated by all Europe and pronounced abominable.
And how can any good man,—any man not wholly thoughtless,—
Any man not willing to be wicked,—enter into such vows?
Is it doubtful whether unjust wars outnumber the just?
In every war between nations one party at least is unjust;
Nor is there any great power but has made many unjust wars;
Wars both unjust and and foolish, no longer defended by any,
Wars of onesided Expediency, or of hot and unseemly haste,
Or of guilty ambition, coveting territory and subjects.
And with facts so awful glaring in our eyes,
Can any one pretend that a war has *ostensibly* God's sanction,
And that men may ravage and burn and slaughter fellow-men,
Merely because it is commanded by a secret Cabinet?—
Oh! but "how else are we to carry on the Government!"
If you cannot stand without brigandage, you had better fall:
But if you desire God's blessing, let martial law be reformed,
Let the Lynch-law of Cabinets be replaced by Judicial Verdict,
And the engagement of a soldier may cease to be brigandage.

THE HARDENED POLITICIAN.

The fool hath said in his heart," We have no law save the law of man."
" Moral law may dwell (saith he,) in the heart of God,
But it cometh not out thence, it reacheth not to us.
No law punisheth but man's law, and no other law hath supremacy.
Come, let me do a clever sin, and men shall praise me.
Let me wound my innocent neighbour, and my king shall exalt me.
Let me argue for the wrong cause, and my party shall admire me.
Let me go through crooked ways, and I shall set the nation straight.
Let me fight for the victory of iniquity, and I shall promote the gospel.
Let me defile my soul with lies, and my mind shall grow stronger;
I will wear the trappings of ambition, and my name shall be proud in History."

If this be wisdom, let it be plainly avowed, and published in books;
Let it be set forth in the pulpits of the clergy, and in the prayers of Parliament.
Let it be boasted of by Christendom, and preached aloud to the heathen:
Let every king and nobleman rejoice in it, and have it taught to his servants,
Until those also enjoy their own sins, whatever the law may not punish,
And serve with eye-service alone, and care only for wages.
Let them study the opinion of their own class, and not the sanctities of conscience,
And practise all unpunishable iniquity, and say to themselves, It is gainful.
Ah! woe to the nation, in which such is the morality of the multitude.

But if no doctrine can be true, which great men dread to whisper,
Which kings hide from their ministers and ministers hide from their kings,
Which preachers would blush to utter, and assembled courtiers to hear,
Which diplomatists craftily dissemble, and none but fools avow;
Then foolish is that heart, which holds the doctrine as true,
And a fool the man who practises it, be he statesman, soldier or king.
For the law of God is relentless, though the common eye fail to track it,
And it hunts down sin revengefully, when the scent has seemed to be lost,
God's punishments are known to us but in part, yet they are not the less real;
And they vindicate in time the supremacy of law, when it is violated,
Nor are conscious sins venial, nor can they be unpunished.
Even by little sins, habitual and deliberate, the conscience is corrupted,
The heart is hardened, the man is degraded, the soul is defiled,
The sight of God is shut out, and his being becomes a tradition,
And the unholy soul is as a fallen angel, who sees no place for himself in heaven.

THE CONSIDERATE POLITICIAN.

Saith the considerate statesman: "This would be a sin only that is necessary:
The world is so imperfect, that it cannot be carried on by purity.
It were better that I needed not to corrupt the electors:
It is sad that I must speak and vote against my heart's consent.
A time, it is to be hoped, shall come, when these things shall be superseded,
But now we must carry on the King's Government as best we may.
God forbid that we forget the duties which each owes to his Party!
Arduous is the task of government, as of war, and admits not common scruples.
Public life is a hard master and demands rigid service;
It orders us to stifle many misgivings, and beware of raw consciences.
But we are improving, and we shall reform: we are made for progress:
We do not bribe as much as we did, nor make quite so many drunkards,
Nor do we take money-bribes in Parliament, nor terrify the juries.
Our appointments to Bishoprics are far better, and so are our clergy:
Little by little we shall amend, and save the rising generation from evil.
Meanwhile, we must not be too scrupulous, or things will get worse;
The wrong party will get into power, who will corrupt the nation,
Will sap our religion by false priests, and do harm to European liberty."

Truly unto *thee* Public Life is a hard master, O Statesman!
It makes of thee a slave, and not a servant; a tool, not a hireling;
Thou yieldest up to it not sinews only and mind, but conscience and soul.
This is necessary for the King's Government, and thou resignest thyself!
O mighty patriot, shall not heaven and earth praise thee?
Hear, O heavens! and give ear, O earth! listen to Sir Henry's sacrifice.
England, perhaps Europe, will be convulsed, unless Sir Henry become false.
To spare us countless griefs, he bears to debase his conscience;
To save us from abounding sin, he volunteers to take sin on himself.
He hardens his conscience a little, lest ours become very hard.

As the scapegoat carried off the sins of Israel, so statesmen our sins,
And their little sins are to shut out great sins, and to fortify us with mercies!
Let thorns produce grapes, and roses flourish on nettles,
If bribery and depravation and falsehood and injustice can bloom into blessing.

TRUTH.

That Truth is not to be observed to enemies in open war,
As not always to madmen, is received for sound morality:
Nor shall I now adventure upon that perplexing argument,

Even if it seem probable that some deeper mind hereafter
Will establish the sterner doctrine that Truth is *never* violable.
Let some hints here suffice, for warning and for protest.

   He who, being captured by an enemy, is exposed to questions,
And from patriotic motives gives false replies,
Loses all his toil, unless he be willing upon demand
To confirm by oath most solemn every plausible falsehood.
If you shrink and shudder before such contingency,
Ask yourself, *why* this shuddering and painful doubt?
Perhaps you feel that Truth is due, not to your enemy,
But to God and to your own soul, and that perjury will defile you?
If it be so when oath is made, is it not the same without oath?
For God is present and hears, whether we invoke him or not,
And to deceive by word or by oath differs not in kind.
If so, will not virtue find other modes of escape,
Which save patriotism without violating truth?
May not a prisoner appeal to the patriotic principle,
And plainly avow that he will not betray his country,—
That no truth is due from him and no truth shall be got from him,
And that he must not be trusted, and it is useless to ask his evidence?
Indeed, after such protest, falsehood itself may seem truth.
He who is bold enough so to act, may need a martyr's spirit,
But he may save patriotism and truth alike,
And may either excite sympathy and win moderation,
Or by his single suffering establish a new right of captives.

   One act or word or falsehood may have its justification,
Real, or else plausible, so as to satisfy most minds,
And save the soul from the degradation of conscious guilt.
But when falsehood is not an act, but a series of acts,
A pervading principle, a tissue of life,
It cannot but debase and weaken the whole man.
Thus notoriously is it with an oppressed enslaved race
Which lives in smouldering warfare, crushed and not reconciled,
With whom fraud becomes patriotism or natural self-defence,
So that fraud is their atmosphere, their breath, their daily life.
If we believe some systems of morality, the fraud is justifiable;
Yet hardly is virtue stable and trustworthy in such men,
Nor will the laxest moralist undervalue the mischief
Engrained in the whole character, where fraud is thus pervading.

   So too, if a man, to attain some secular promotion,
Perform one religious act contrary to his heart's consent,

(As some have qualified for office by sacred bread and wine,
And others by subscription of articles and by oaths to statutes,)
Such falsehood is a sin and an evil, and in itself indefensible;
Yet the more isolated from the daily life, the less its corrupting force;
Especially if half-forgotten, and buried from public consciousness.
But if daily duties recall the pledge, the falsehood is a daily act.
And even without pledge, daily dissimulation taints the character;
Chiefly when it is dissimulation dictated by *fear*.
He who represses his solemn convictions from erring philanthropy,
May weaken his own character, but does not debase it.
But he who every day and all his life suppresses truth through *fear*,
May hardly escape an inward and terrible degradation.

Consider the hired advocate, whose duty is one-sided,
Who proclaims plainly that he studies his client's interest,
And from whom none expect judicial and fair reasonings.
If such a man fail of truth by suppressions only,
Displaying a partial argument, such as fairly deserves account,
And leaving the opposite view to be unfolded by others;
Under such modest restraint, he may retain delicacy of conscience,
As we sometimes see in men assuredly noble of heart.
But if, claiming the license of his craft, he plunge into free falsehoods,
Though only when in Court, and only where avowedly an advocate;
Truly he may avoid reproach by pleading the sharp limits of his freedom,
Yet will he not avoid debasement and blunting of the conscience,
Nor ever retain a judgment severe and sensitive to truth:
But he is in training to become a shameless and unscrupulous politician,
Ever false and plausible and pliant to public crime.

And oh, how pernicious, how indefensible to fresh minds,
Is the habitual untruth which many public men practise!
In dealing not with enemies, but with countrymen and coadjutors,
They profess to be honourable, yet account frank speech a folly,
And pretend that dissimulation is necessary for Government,
And that the misarrangements brought in by policy are sacred,
Worthy to be maintained by hypocrisies and endless evil.
Thus the candidate for votes disguises his heart to the people,
And trusted ministers disguise their convictions to the parliament,
Arguing against their own judgment with crafty sophistry;
Or garble public facts by suppression and by false colouring,
If they do not even step onward into direct false evidence.
And others carry into Opposition the immoralities of Office,
Being notoriously without truth, true only to their ambition,

Yet are not thought unfitted for the highest places of the State.
Who can expect righteous rule, or hope to escape retribution,
Until reputed truthfulness be essential in high magistracy,
Equally as in courteous life, where no chicanery is endured?

OATHS AND SOLEMN AFFIRMATIONS.

An Oath consists not in any set form of words,
Nor in any deed or gesture, nor in the utterance of curses,
(As some have held it to require a conditional self-cursing,)
But it is a solemn statement made as under God's cognizance
By one reminded of his presence and avowing that he remembers it.
Atheists cannot avow this, yet they can make Solemn Affirmation.
And because many men are prone to be careless and light-minded,
Speaking without seriousness and without measuring their words,
Oftentimes it is hard to bind them to sober and strict truth,
Unless definite and solemn form be used, which admits of no mistake,
Pledging their conscience and their honour in utmost gravity.
Cruel and stupid have been many legal enactments,
Which overlook the substance of oaths and enforce their shadow,
And punish over-scrupulous Christians and refuse justice to Atheists:
Nor are all the injustices by any means yet removed.
Yet the whole controversy would vanish as an empty cloud,
Did not bigotry care more for the outside than for the reality.
Scarcely would one find the difference between Solemn Affirmation and Oath,
If the process were duly administered by a religious Judge,
Who should remind him who swears of a God listening to his words,
And after declaring the sin of treachery and its legal penalties,
Should call upon him, by whatever is sacred to him in earth or heaven,
To bear truthful witness or give truthful verdict.
Assuredly no Atheist would refuse this summons,
Nor would it have less solemnity than the kissing of a book,
Coupled with four glib monosyllables from a heartless voice:
Nor would Perjury be then less guilty, or its penalty be less,
Nor the bond of honour be slighter, nor yet the shame from its breach.

Oaths need to be extended, not to be abolished,
Since the State ought to be religious, and public duty sacred.
Oaths belong to the decision of all high and sacred right,
As between man and man, so yet more between nation and nation,

And to engagements of duty between magistrates and subjects.
Oaths of Allegiance, of Coronation or of magisterial Office,
Oaths of affidavit and of witness, as of forensic Jury,
Oaths of solemn Treaty, as likewise of military obedience,
Have been approved deliberately in all well-ordered States,
Christian or Mussulman, or of earlier ages, far and wide:
And herein a broad and fruitful principle is conceded.
If many men are such as to be biassed by party and by convenience,
And by loves and hatreds, and by selfishness, to the neglect of duty,
Unless tied down to a solemn and well defined avowal,
Consecrated to Honour and to Conscience and to Religion;
But, when bound by these pledges, can better be trusted:
And if, by reason of this, the oaths above named are expedient;—
Then equally expedient are oaths in cases parallel to these:
As, not only when a jury has to award twenty or ten shillings,
But when a Cabinet or a Parliament has to pronounce on foreign rights:
Nor only in interpreting the words of some ancient Treaty,
But in pronouncing Sacred Right where no treaty may exist.
Vast indeed is the field, wherein the Just is now overruled,
Both at home and abroad, in favour of crooked policy,
Not so much because public men are consciously unprincipled,
As because no sacred formula awakens their conscience to duty.

 Every high public trust is committed with religious sanction,
And is duly guarded by the solemnity of an oath.
Then what reason can be pleaded, except love of malversation,
Why every one entrusted with "Patronage," in State or Church,
Should not on each appointment solemnly avow that he selects*
      the Fittest Man he can find?

CLEANLINESS.

 All ancient religions embraced Cleanliness in their precepts,
And prescribed minutely concerning animal-purity,
Shrinking not from details unpleasant for public reading.
Nor was public decorum hurt; for then surely as now
Such passages of law were little obtruded promiscuously.
And Cleanliness not only is allied to personal health,

---

* As in the old Roman oath of office, to promote *optimum quemque*.

But closely concerns all our neighbours and society.
Some forms of impurity make the body an annoyance,
Or even noxious and a source of pestilence;
Such is the uncleanness of the pauperized, the reckless, the brutal.
But other forms of the same are more selfish and more guilty,
Precisely because they do not harm the individual,
Nor betray themselves in his person, yet are a pestilence to others.
With excellent reason then did ancient religion judge,
In denouncing with authority every such negligence as a sin,
And in driving away from the public throng (sacred or civil)
Every leper or unclean person who might spread a dangerous taint.

   But when religion urged Cleanliness so authoritatively,
That it could not be more authoritative for Justice and Truth,
And zeal for ceremonies spread, and men made display of Holiness
By various outward purity, forgetting the inward man;
Then the precepts of cleanliness became disguised and mistaken:
And one class of men extolled ceremonious purity
As of celestial value,—the more artificial the more divine,—
And despised foreign virtue, which neglected such precepts;
While another class of men decried ceremonial purity,
And reproved all religious enforcement of cleanliness,
As confounding inward holiness with the fictitious outside.
Nay, reversing asceticism, many marvellously went forward
Into admiration of filthiness and of bodily neglect,
As denoting the true saint, raised above things earthly,
Bent to renounce or to humiliate all that vulgar minds cherish.
We have outgrown *both* errors; yet our system remains mutilated.
Religion fears to descend, and to meddle in things extraneous,
If now, as of old, she resume the care of cleanliness.
The State interferes in extreme cases, feebly, fitfully;
For Laws unseconded by Morals are irresolute and ill-executed.
Yet the poorest, the uneducated, the unpolished, the millions,
Endure misery, debasement, fevers, death,
Partly from their own ignorance, partly from men's avarice,
In want of land to live on and of air to breathe:
(For Land has been made private, where it ought to be public;)
And in turn becoming blunted to the sense of uncleanness,
And hopeless of a better state, they make no effort for a better,
But being defiled, become defilers, and aid the public mischief.
And many call helplessly on Parliament and on the Queen's Ministers,
Overworking the central machine which is overworked already,

While Philanthropy does a little, but Religion fears to speak
And add her solemn sanction, to forbid and to command.
   Civilization is coeval with the dominion of Law,
Which bridles the violent, be he chief or common man,
Establishing fixed principles approved by the ablest.
And everywhere it is agreed that pure Air and pure Water,
Needful to life and health, must be held sacred by all,
And that land must belong to all, so far as is essential to life.
To pollute the healthful streams for one's own convenience,
Is a crime hated and punished, alike among the barbarous
And in all earlier civilization: and is denounced by religion
As an impious iniquity, a hideous and cruel guilt,
Until the organs of religion are confederate with Mammon.
Now,* month by month, some pure stream is spoiled
For the convenience of private industry and to increase gain.
Even on the mountain side, the cottager, who dwells aloft,
Defiles the stream to the damage of those below,
And the traveller dares not drink, if he espies cabins above.
The workers of wealthy mines poison glorious mountain torrents,
Drugging them with lead or copper to save themselves petty trouble;
And the peasant groans in secret or regards it as a "landed right,"
And after some lapse of time the law counts the right valid;
Or the poor are soothed by wages and the rich smother the law,
Or enact new statutes, which sanction their odiousness
And override the common law by which they were condemned.
So also vast cities grow up, accustomed to self-defilements,
As the pig, walled in a sty, pollutes his own bed.
Such loathsome evil have Terror and Avarice enacted,
Cooping into wretched towns those who should overspread the country,
And changing God's pure rivers into filthy drains.
And clever men, who deplore this, and proffer sanitary aid,
Bid us trust in new sewerage and in their artful construction,
While they inveigh against the work of clever predecessors,
Whose drains are half stagnant, or are mixed with the wells,
From which wretched thousands drink pestilence in the dry weather.
Thus underneath our cities, by curious and perishing art,
A new city is built, of Tartarean loathsomeness,
A network of brick-bowels, which perpetually decay,
Yet give no sign of decay, duly to warn those above;

---

* Written in 1857.

Being a trap of pestilence to the following generation,
Which may moralize over *our* ill-workmanship and stupidity
Just as *we* moralize now over the stupidity of the preceding.
Nor in a crowded city permeated by countless drains
Can any wells be counted on as permanently safe;
Nor can any one say, how long this or that spot shall be pure,
When blasts of pestilence are necessarily breathed up,
Or must burst open the drains if refused an exit.
Where Nature is destroyed and Artifice enthroned,
And pure Air and Water alike need to be bought by money,
The rich man migrates ever, as each spot in turn is corrupted,
But the poor remains of necessity, though the ground teem with disease.
Surely our contrivances are but as Crutches to a lame man,
Necessary alleviations, but not normal and desirable.
New principles are essential, the fruit of freer thought,
Before Cleanliness and Health can be normal and rightful.

   Cleanliness and Health are conditions of general Virtue,
Conditions of Contentment, removing misery from Poverty.
Cleanliness and Health are the birthright of every savage:
Surely that "civilization" is barbarous which steals them from the poor.
Why should not Religion, now equally as of old,
Lift up her voice for every right of man,
And enforce duty on individuals, whether for body or mind?
Man's conscience responds to every such faithful utterance,
Nor would the ministers of religion long protest in vain.

FOOD AND DRINK.

   The poorer part of mankind perforce eat what they can get:
The rich in most countries eat what best pleases their palate.
When necessity constrains to certain food, and no choice is given,
No moral rule can exist, except as to the quantity eaten.
But when a choice between this food and that food is open,
Our choice should conduce to our own health of body and mind,
Next, to our neighbours' welfare and to public convenience;
Nor may the rights of other animals justly be forgotten.
To please the palate, cannot fitly, as an end, be made primary.
Taste, within certain limits is changeable and docile:

When our food is conformed to Nature, Nature is satisfied,
And the food generally becomes palatable, when good of its kind.
Taste ought not to lead the way: rather will Taste follow;
Though, when moral claims are satisfied, private taste may be indulged.
But for national welfare Food well chosen is of great avail.
Man, by nature naked and unarmed, is a tropical animal,
Who finds his food wild on fruit-trees pleasant and many.
But driven out from such Paradise, he roams into climates less lavish,
Where the earth awaits her tiller, and proffers scantier nourishment.
Here barbarous man, as hunter or keeper of cattle,
Becomes a flesh-eater, familiar with blood,
Else in rivers, lakes or sea he entraps fish for his food:
Until by collective force crops may safely be guarded,
And with grain, pulse and roots the garners are amply stored.
At length by human care fruit also and green crops are raised.

In every region an era comes, sooner or later,
When a national diet on flesh-meat causes enormous waste;
When an increase of cattle means a decrease or arrest of mankind,
And an increase of human population requires a decrease of cattle.
That condition will at length be universal; then men must perforce,
Chiefly if not wholly, be nourished on fruits of earth.
In most well-peopled nations we see the tendency active:
In China already it is pre-eminent and notorious.
"None of us liveth to himself and none of us dieth to himself,"
Eloquently says a Christian apostle; propounding a fertile maxim:
"But whether we live, we live to the Lord,
Or whether we die, we die to the Lord;
Therefore let us even eat and drink to the glory of God."
How then can man increase glory to the Highest?
By living not for himself, but for the benefit of his fellowmen.
While by food and drink he nourishes himself and satisfies nature,
Let him so eat and so drink, if he be richer than the majority,
That neither may his greater wealth damage the market of the many,
Nor lead their covetings astray into hurtful channels.
Also let not his dainty appetite cause cruelty to animals:
He is lord of this world; why should he be its tyrant?
As to drink, what can defend fiery narcotic liquors,
Which harden food in the stomach and arrest digestion?
Liquors, which to every nation that drinks them habitually
Have ever hitherto been a curse, most fatal.
For in every population abound the young and the weak of mind,

Who, if such drinks be customary, are enticed into the gravest evil :
For, the mind and the morals are affected, before the foot is unsteady.
Nor is the evil confined to the drinker himself,
But on great numbers beside entails misery, vice and ruin,
Causing pauperism and orphanhood, violent crime and insanity.
Who then can deny, that here Paul's maxim applies,
" Eat ye not, drink ye not, if it occasion your brother's fall," ?—
Religious lawgivers of the East, by their prohibition of strong drinks,
Have benefited, on a scale immeasurable, hundreds of millions.

RIGHTS OF ANIMALS.

How pleasant is it to see beautiful creatures, otherwise wild,
Become tame and trustful to the hand of man,
Or at least not terrified by his near approaches !
As when the gentle fallow deer loves to be fondled,
And the hare and the pheasant are not scared,
Or the stork calmly builds its nest on the housetop.
The life of such animals may be taken for man's need,
Yet it is not indifferent in what way it be taken ;
Whether so as only to cut short the days of the individual,
Or so as also to distress and terrify the living,
Chasing them from pleasant haunts into distant refuge less hospitable,
And filling them with terror of man their enemy.
The more intelligent the animal, the worse the infliction ;
For he remembers both the causes of danger and its neighbourhoods,
And by his sagacity shuns new encounter with the more powerful.
Thus the beaver is driven from his rivers and favourite pools.
Thus the gentle seal, massacred in heaps by sailors,
Forsakes milder seas and its well-known creeks,
Plunging into drearier mist and further ice,
Which punish not undeservedly the too relentless persecutor,
Who thought but of momentary gain by promiscuous slaughter,
And, slighting all rights of animals, was unwise for his own future.
  That all living things have some rights, no one will deny ;
For wanton cruelty is universally condemned :
Yet the limits of their rights have been scarcely discussed,

Nor the diverse rights of diverse animals
Under circumstances diverse, such as tame and wild.
The tame creature which receives and gives affection
Is with most humane persons a sacred life;
Nor will many approve to slaughter a pet lamb
Or a much fondled gazelle, for daintiness and avarice;
Though for any real necessity the same cannot be disapproved.
Not but that it is well pressed by advocates of Vegetarianism,
That for taking animal life a grave justification is needed.
If health, strength and comfort, with equal longevity,
Can be sustained on other food, especially with less human labour,
No reason for depriving animals of sweet life remains,
Much less for wounding and killing with cruelty
Such creatures as have exquisite sensitiveness equal to ours.
No excess of birds need be feared, if we let alone their natural foes.
Nor reply thou, that thus also they will be cruelly killed.
The hawk and the weasel kill with certainty and with ease.

 The cattle that multiply under man's care and protection,
Who in some sense may be said to have bestowed life upon them;
Such cattle, if not admitted into personal attachment,
Nor endowed with sagacity to foresee or to remember deaths,
Are slain for man's use without moral mischief,
On condition that the slaughter be sudden and complete.

 Not but that even here, caution may justly be entered,
Against *so* inflicting death as to wound those who live.
To kill a calf while the mother will grieve for it,
Does not merely shorten a life, but tortures maternal feeling,
Which exists in the cow less intelligently than in the woman,
Yet not less truly or less unfailingly:
And even if man's nobler life be well fed by animal life,
Yet daintiness of appetite, though in a man, is less noble
Than maternal affection, though it be but in a cow:
And a better morality than that hitherto called Christian
Will hereafter enact a sharper limit of our rights over the animal.

 In fact over wild creatures, which man has never protected
Nor fed, nor in any way reared, we have no direct claim;
For neither strength over weakness nor cunning over simplicity
Gives any validity of right, except for protection and government.
But the creatures which exist without mutual affection,
Having neither family life nor maternal sentiment,
Living for themselves alone, grieving for none,

Have not even the rudiments of morality or of moral rights:
And where life is wholly unmoral, we are free to take it.
Thus man captures and devours the fish of seas and rivers,
As innocently as the same fish devour one another,
Violating no tender affection nor engendering moral evil.

 Less clear by far is the case with animals intelligent and affectionate,
Which love their own comrades and resent their wrongs ;
As the troops of walrus and of seal assemble for vengeance,
If but one of their own band has been harmfully assailed ;
And mourn over the slaughtered, and piteously remember the place :—
Creatures sensible and kind, not less sagacious than dogs,
Curious of man's ways and of the sweet sounds of music,
So that, but for their marine life, sea-dogs would be our faithful friends.
Surely, to harass these creatures is not without its evil
In the eye of the great God who inspires their mutual love.

 Nor can other destructive commercial hunting be approved.
As, where the majestic bison ranges the prairie,
Cut off by wild forest and swamp from inhabited lands ;
The hunters, incited by trade, kill the noble game without measure,
Strewing the ground with (it may be) four hundred huge carcases,
And carry away but four hundred wretched *tongues!*
Many such are the enormities where Law cannot reach.

 While human tribes shall live on the grounds of the bear and wolf,
Driven thither by tyrannies or detained by ignorance
And by bodily habits half assimilated to the brutal,
So long the wild seal must perish for the wild man.
But the times of man's misgovernment are not to be eternal,
Nor can eternal morality be framed out of transitory facts ;
And those who have learnt well that the Moral is higher than the Material,
Will not despise tender affection though in the bosom of ape or bear.

 On the Galipagos Islands, where men have not dwelt permanently,
In respect of birds and beasts, is a modern garden of Eden,
Where birds settle on the buckets while men are carrying them.
Oh how great the delight to live among birds thus tame !
What man is so void of sentiment as rather to wish to eat them ?

 The Turk, the Arab, the Indian,—men individually rude,—
Are often taught by religion to revere God's gift of life,
And to abhor destroying life save for security or need.
To enjoy acts of slaughter, and the sport of killing,
Belonged (once upon a time) to none but wild barbarians,
In whom hunting had engendered a love of mere destruction.

It is reserved for modern times, and pre-eminently for Christians,
That humane and refined men should sport with deeds of blood,
Killing and wounding the timid, the gentle, the beautiful,
Not for food nor even for daintiness, but for the pride of skill.
What tender and thoughtful heart will call such pastime pleasure,
And think without compunction over the lingerings of the wounded?

ADORATION.

Religion with many men stops short in a *Fear* of God,
And in a sense of the *Duty* to thank him for his Providence.
Such religion is apt to be a limited and a dry service,
Alive chiefly at certain times or even in certain places.
Yet it is not to be despised, nor even disparaged,
But to be approved and exhorted, and persuasively led onward.
  With others Religion is founded on personal *Gratitude*,
Conscious of private benefits, of peculiar advantages,
Both in outward circumstance and far more in things spiritual;
When the man feels how much has been given and forgiven,
And is grateful for Mercy, and wonders why he is distinguished.
This is a warmer and more generous principle,
Ripening into the love of God and into holy communion,
Though in its cruder form it endanger much personal conceit.
Yet it pervades the whole soul, and makes religion a life,
And fuses into unity the secular and the spiritual.
  As generous and more noble is the religion of those,
Who, forgetting self, adore the most High for his Holiness,
Rejoicing that he is Good in himself and to all,
And that Goodness is eternal, all-mighty, all-ruling.
Such *Absolute Devotion* is higher than Gratitude,
Warmer also than a sense of Duty, and less outwearying;
Yet it includes within itself both Gratitude and Duty,
And holds up the high ideal of perfect Holiness,
And purifies the soul and shames away petty vices,
And enlarges it to embrace all God's creatures in its kindliness.
  This is the true way to overcome Sin and the World;
Not by dwelling on our sins or depreciating things outward,

But by pre-occupying the heart with better aspirations.
If, consciousness of weakness and of past sin discourage thee,
Shun the occasions of sin, but let not repentance linger over it.
As though to God and to the universe thy sin had been deadly hurt;
But if thou know thyself defiled, then praise God for his purity,
Turn from thy sinful weakness to remember his holy strength;
And if thou hast any hate of sin, rejoice that sin cannot last,
But that thy sins and all men's sins shall be conquered and overruled
By that glorious majesty, which silent and unseen
Guides its eternal counsels toward perfection and bliss unutterable.

 Whatever heart sincerely can glorify God's holiness,
Needs no permission or license other than its actual power;
And by such adoration the force of sin is quelled,
And the feeble struggler is raised into the hopeful saint.
Many might well pray less, if they would praise God more,
Praise him, both for what they are and what he is to them,
And also more signally for what he is to all.
Adoration of God is the universal and final religion,
That which shall hereafter unite the Mussulman* and the Christian,
The man and the angel, in this world or in whatever world.

---

* Dr. Henry Barth, the celebrated African traveller, appears to have made the simple and important discovery, that a Christian may disarm the bigotry of a Mussulman by chanting with him the first chapter of the Koran, a chapter to which both Christian and Jew give a hearty assent. Might not this assume social and political importance in India?

EPILOGUS.

We praise thee in thy power, O God!
We praise thee in thy sanctity.
We praise thee who reignest in the furthest heavens,
We praise thee who dwellest in our inmost souls,
Our Lord and hidden Comforter.
No voice can duly proclaim thy greatness,
No heart can comprehend thy goodness,
Oh thou Father of all our spirits.
The longings of the spirit are inexhaustible:
Only thou canst fill the heart.
When it is empty and aching for thee,
Hungering and thirsting for thy righteousness,
Thou visitest it with peace unspeakable.
With thee there is no misery to the distressed;
But sorrow is hallowed and pain is sweetened,
And hardship is assuaged and fear calmed.
For, thine own nature is blessedness,
And thou makest thy worshippers blessed.
   Yea, blessed is thy presence, O Lord most Holy!
Blessed is it to dwell with thee and to know thee,
To rest on thee and to serve thee.
Blessed shall the nations be, when thy glory is recognized,
When all who love thee unite to succour and raise the weak,
When men of all climes and colours know their union.
Meanwhile, enable us to discern and love thy servants,
Under whatever strange name or false creed they are hidden.
Strengthen us in life or death, in this and in every life,
To be thine in fact, as we are thine in right;
To obey cheerfully, to strive loyally,
To suffer meekly, to enjoy thankfully.
So shall we love thee while we live, and partake of thy joy,
And triumph over sorrow, and fulfil thy work,
And be numbered with thy saints, and die on thy bosom.

LIST OF WORKS
BY
F. W. NEWMAN,
PUBLISHED BY

TRÜBNER & CO., 57 & 59, LUDGATE HILL, LONDON.

THE ODES OF HORACE translated into unrhymed metre, with Introduction and ample Notes. 8vo., cloth. 5s.

THE ILIAD OF HOMER faithfully translated into unrhymed metre. Second Edition. Royal 8vo., cloth. 1871. 10s. 6d.

HOMERIC TRANSLATION: a reply to Professor MATTHEW ARNOLD. 2s. 6d.

THE TEXT OF THE IGUVINE INSCRIPTIONS, with Interlinear Latin Translations and Notes. 8vo. 2s.

HIAWATHA: rendered into Latin, with abridgement. 12mo. 2s. 6d.

TRANSLATIONS OF ENGLISH POETRY INTO LATIN VERSE. Crown 8vo., cloth, pp. xiv. and 202. 6s.

ORTHOEPY; or, a Simple Mode of Accenting English, for the advantage of Foreigners and all Learners. 1s.

A HANDBOOK OF MODERN ARABIC, consisting of a Practical Grammar, with numerous examples, dialogues, and newspaper extracts, in a European type. In one vol., crown 8vo., pp. 212, cloth. 6s.

"This manual is peculiarly adapted to render the earlier stages in the acquisition of the Arabic language much easier than they are ordinarily proved to be. For by an exact system of transliteration of that alphabet into easy equivalents, it saves the student the double perplexity of having to contend, at once, with a strange language and a strange character; and while familiarizing him with the sound of the more common words and constructions, it insensibly leads him to the knowledge of the original mode of writing them. To those who wish to acquire and speak modern Arabic, this work, by the singular pains taken to define and enforce the exact sounds of the spoken language, offers advantages very far surpassing those of the most celebrated grammars of the learned idioms."—DR. J. NICHOLSON, Penrith.

A DICTIONARY OF MODERN ARABIC. 1. Anglo-Arabic Dictionary. 2. Anglo-Arabic Vocabulary. 3. Arabo-English Dictionary. The Arabic words printed in a type substantially that of Europe. In 2 vols., crown 8vo., pp. xvi. and 376—464, cloth. £1 1s.

MISCELLANIES; chiefly Addresses, Academical and Historical. 8vo., pp. iv. and 356, cloth. 7s. 6d.

ON THE RELATIONS OF FREE KNOWLEDGE TO MORAL SENTIMENT. 8vo., sewed, pp. 24. 1s.

THE RELATIONS OF PROFESSIONAL TO LIBERAL KNOWLEDGE. 8vo., sewed, pp. 30. 1859. 1s.

THE DIFFICULTIES OF ELEMENTARY GEOMETRY, especially those which concern the straight line, the plane, and the theory of parallels. 8vo., boards, pp. viii. and 144. 5s.

LECTURE ON THE PHILOSOPHICAL CLASSIFICATION OF NATIONAL INSTITUTIONS. 8vo., pp. 24. 6d.

THE RELATION OF PHYSIOLOGY TO SEXUAL MORALS. 8vo., pp. 42, sewed. 1s.

LECTURES ON POLITICAL ECONOMY. Crown 8vo., pp. 342, cloth. 5s.

EUROPE OF THE NEAR FUTURE. With Three Letters on the Franco-German War. Crown 8vo., pp. 64, cloth. 2s.

A HISTORY OF THE HEBREW MONARCHY from the Administration of Samuel to the Babylonian Captivity. Third Edition. Large post 8vo., cloth. 8s. 6d.

CATHOLIC UNION: Essays towards a Church of the Future, as the Organization of Philanthropy. Crown 8vo., pp. 114, cloth. 3s. 6d.

THE SOUL, ITS SORROWS AND ITS ASPIRATIONS: an Essay towards the Natural History of the Soul, as the True Basis of Theology. Seventh Edition. Crown 8vo., pp. 174, cloth. 3s. 6d.

PHASES OF FAITH; or, Passages from the History of my Creed. Sixth Edition; with Reply to Professor HENRY ROGERS, Author of the "Eclipse of Faith." Crown 8vo., pp. 212, cloth. 3s. 6d.

A DISCOURSE AGAINST HERO-MAKING IN RELIGION. 8vo. 1s.

Also, abridged *by the same*, with KOSSUTH's express sanction, KOSSUTH'S AMERICAN SPEECHES. Post 8vo., pp. 388. 5s.

MORAL INFLUENCE OF LAW. A Lecture in Finsbury Chapel.

The following, also from the pen of Professor F. W. NEWMAN, *are*

Published by Mr. THOMAS SCOTT, 11, The Terrace, Farquhar Road, Upper Norwood, S.E.

and may be obtained through Messrs. TRÜBNER *& Co.,* 57 *and* 59, *Ludgate Hill, London, E.C.*

AGAINST HERO-MAKING IN RELIGION. 6d.

JAMES AND PAUL. 6d.

ON THE CAUSES OF ATHEISM. 6d.

ON THE RELATIONS OF THEISM TO PANTHEISM; and ON THE GALLA RELIGION. 3d.

ON THE HISTORICAL DEPRAVATION OF CHRISTIANITY. 3d.

REPLY TO A LETTER FROM AN EVANGELICAL LAY PREACHER. 3d.

THE BIGOT AND THE SCEPTIC. 6d.

THE CONTROVERSY ABOUT PRAYER. 3d.

THE DIVERGENCE OF CALVINISM FROM PAULINE DOCTRINE. 3d.

THE RELIGIOUS WEAKNESS OF PROTESTANTISM. 6d.

THE TRUE TEMPTATION OF JESUS. 6d.

THOUGHTS ON THE EXISTENCE OF EVIL. 3d.

www.ingramcontent.com/pod-product-compliance
Lightning Source LLC
Chambersburg PA
CBHW032151160426
43197CB00008B/861